D1321474

AUTOMOTIVE CHEAP TRICKS AND SPECIAL F/X

By Craig Fraser

Published By Airbrush Action, Inc.

ACKNOWLEDGMENTS

We would like to express our appreciation to those who contributed to this book.

Designer: **Michele DeBlock**
Editors: **Laurette Koserowski, Cliff Stieglitz, Jennifer Bohanan & Kate Priest**
Production Manager: **Michele DeBlock**
Cover Design: **Ed Hettig**

Books are available for bulk purchases at special discounts. For information, contact Airbrush Action.

First edition published 1999.
Second printing 2003.
Third printing 2004.
Fourth printing 2005.

Published in the United States of America by:
Airbrush Action, Inc.
P.O. Box 438
Allenwood, NJ 08720
Tel: (732) 223-7878
Fax: (732) 223-2855
E-Mail: ceo@airbrushaction.com
www.airbrushaction.com

ISBN: 0-9637336-1-3

Printed in Singapore

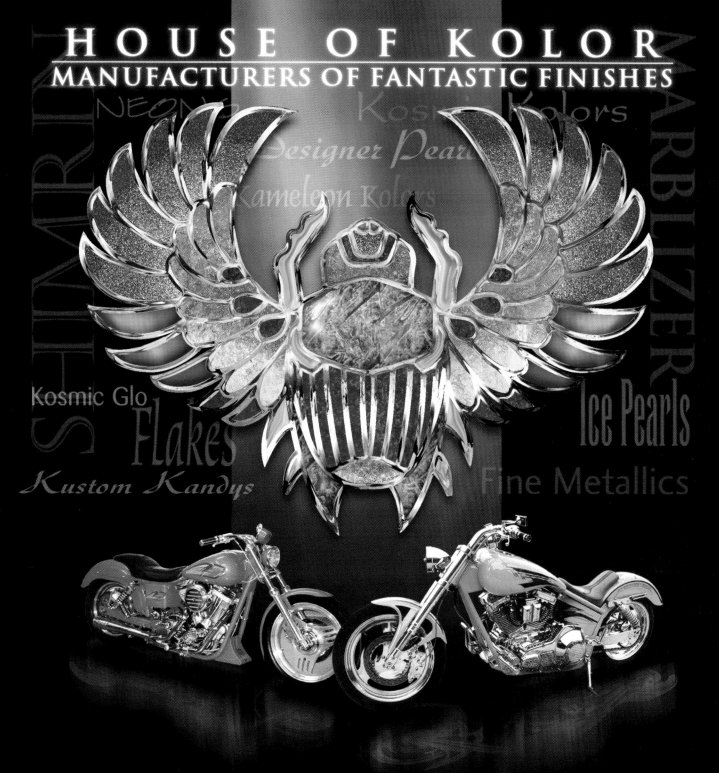

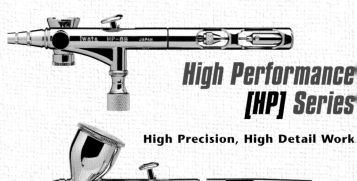

TABLE OF CONTENTS

INTRODUCTION
"ZEN AND THE ART OF AUTOMOTIVE AIRBRUSHING"

BY CRAIG FRASER

In this world of radical paint jobs and mind-numbing graphics, it has become the general consensus that man cannot live by single color alone. It used to be that if you had graphics, or anything with four or more colors, your paint job was considered radical. But now colors aren't enough–we need F/X (effects). One of the newest concepts to hit the shops in the last few years is the return of the airbrush to the automotive painting scene. Drop shadows, highlights, marblizing, and Van Halens are terms that are becoming all too familiar to the painter and striper. With just a little ingenuity and a few stolen signpainting tricks (not to mention some vintage *Hot Rod* magazines), painters can spice up their graphics with their own bag of F/X.

In fact, the techniques that I teach in this book are similar to those popular back in the 1960s and early 1970s—the height of the kustom painting genre. The only difference between then and now is not the tricks, but the way painters present them. If you stay on top of industry trends, you can modify your work to give the public what it wants; if you're clever enough, you can even influence the trends yourself.

I've made the demos in this book fairly product indeterminate, since many of the automotive paints only have a functional life span of about three to five years before they become obsolete or just plain illegal. For those of you already in the automotive paint or kustom industry, you know what I mean. For those of you just starting out, you must understand the necessity of continuing education on the use of materials.

I mention a number of House of Kolor products only because they're what I currently use in the studio and in our shop at Kal Koncepts. But the techniques and demos remain the same, no matter what products you use. I do, however, recommend the use of automotive urethanes, primarily transparent toners. Our shop has used different brands during the past six years, but our use of transparent toners has remained constant.

For veterans in the painting industry (or veteran readers of *Airbrush Action*), some of the demos will be familiar—a perfect example of how the techniques and tricks I used six years ago are still going strong today. The only difference between then and now is the materials I use. Because of this, I've modified the demos to make them more current. By being more color descriptive than product descriptive, this book won't go the way of the dodo bird, even if we are painting with soybean-based paints in the future. (No, this isn't inside information. I just made it up. But if the industry's history is an indication, it's anyone's guess as to where the chemists will take us.)

I hope you find this book useful. And if it saves you a bit of time and stomach lining, then it accomplished what it intended. I'll just close with my own philosophy on kustom painting: The competitive airbrush industry is much like a foot race. People may show up randomly, shine for a while, and disappear. The rules may change, but the race is never really over. The only way you can stay ahead is to keep moving. No matter how talented someone may be, he'll still be a few paces behind the one who keeps running. In short, the only people who are outdated and left behind in this industry are the ones who sit on their asses.

Paint to Live, Live to Paint.

AIR SYNDICATE

"The Three Guyz": Craig, D-Bob, and K-Daddy. Post-sixties "Dolemite" wear.

Craig, Cliff Stieglitz, and D-Bob at the Grand Opening of the new Kal Koncepts/Air Syndicate Showroom in 1998. Be sure to come to our next Annual Open House and every one after that.

Chris's immaculate Nissan at the Open House, as seen on the cover of *Minitruckin'* magazine.

D-Bob demonstrating the joy of spraying coarse metalflake.

Craig doing his Shakespeare soliloquy: "Alas poor urethane. I knew him Horatio."

D-Bob ready to remove Craig's camera.

Chuck Hartsfield's boat after getting the Kal Koncepts treatment. Urethane use at its best—155 MPH!

The Chop-Shop van before someone else bought it and repainted it. (We won't go there.) Needless to say, it gets no magazine coverage now. (A moment of silence, please, for the death of a good paint job.)

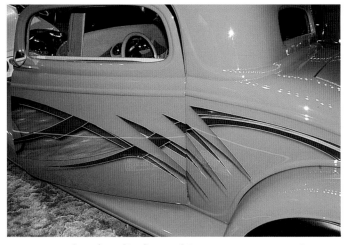

An example of radical graphics on a conservative Street Rod. The judges seemed to like it!

The two-sided Spawn bike.

The other side of the Spawn bike. (Who said you can only have one paint job per vehicle? Tooky wanted both on his bike, so he got it!)

An example of the pioneering of automotive urethanes on aluminum panels for fine art. It's not just for cars anymore!

A future kustomizer in the making. Gabrielle Giuliano (Dion's daughter) cruisin' her new ride. No vehicle is safe from paint at KKAS!

K-Daddy in one of his isocyanate episodes.

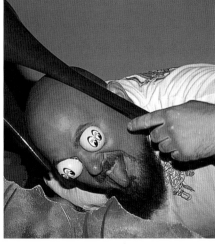

K-Daddy in another one of his isocyanate episodes.

K-Daddy in yet another one of his isocyanate episodes.

FOREWORD

The first time I met Craig Fraser, he was doing an airbrush demonstration, and around him was an array of painted motorcycle parts and helmets displaying his workmanship. It stopped me dead in my tracks — I was profoundly impressed with the quality of the work I saw.

Our friendship began with that meeting, and I started to learn more and more about Craig Fraser. With less than a decade in the airbrushing field, he has been an innovator who fully understands his media, the products he uses, and how to bring those products into the automotive customizing arena.

Craig knows what works — and what doesn't — in many different areas. He's been very beneficial to House of Kolor, and his input regarding our products has been priceless. One of the things I admire about Craig is his candor; when he is unhappy about a product he is using, he's honest about it. That kind of frankness is hard to find, but Craig demands products that work, and are worth his time, effort and expense.

A true friend to the airbrushing community, Craig's efforts have helped tune us into the world of auto refinishing. For example, he has experimented with products in ways that never occurred to us and, as a result, he has pioneered new uses for many of the items we produce.

As a teacher, he is patient, understanding, articulate and doesn't use technical jargon that confuses his audience. Instead, he uses everyday language so an average person just coming into the field who attends one of Craig's seminars will have a full understanding. I've watched him work on video; he hides nothing. That's one of the great things about Craig — there are no secrets that he will not reveal about the work that he does. He wants you to succeed. He genuinely wants to help each of his "students" come away from his seminars with the ability to do the best work. To find a teacher with that kind of generosity, depth, and skill is rare indeed.

Craig Fraser is an icon in the world of airbrushing. He frequently contributes to a host of publications, demonstrating exactly how to complete a project successfully. In the early part of my 40+ year career of "kustom" painting, we used to guard secrets, refusing to share them with others because the knowledge was hard-earned. It was, and is, unusual to find someone with the integrity to lay it all out for anyone who wants to learn. Craig is a unique artist, and I am positive his book will enlighten you on a range of critical issues and show you just how he accomplishes his works of art.

Enjoy it. It's going to be a great ride.

Jon Kosmoski
Founder, House of Kolor Kustom Paint Products

PREFACE

Have I got a story! At the 2nd Annual Coast Airbrush Party, an airbrusher, who had just popped in on the automotive scene, decided to try his luck with an artist's booth. He had recently returned to the country and decided to give airbrushing a shot before beginning a career in architecture (for which he had a college degree).

On the second day of the party, the airbrusher was in his booth working on a demo hood mural. Suddenly he noticed an older man with a long, gray ponytail trying to catch his eye. The man approached the booth with his wife and began admiring the portfolios of helmets and motorcycle tanks.

"Man! I've never seen work like this before," the man said. "You're really good. Where are you from?" The airbrusher thanked him for the generous compliment, handed him a business card and replied, "Bakersfield."

The man looked stunned for a moment. "I've lived in Bakersfield for most of my life and I've never heard of you. When did you show up?"

The airbrusher replied that he had been gone for a while, but had actually grown up in Bakersfield and had done T-shirt and illustration work before leaving for college.

"Well, I've never heard of you. And if I had seen you or your work, I definitely would have remembered," the man insisted.

"Do you remember about 18 years ago, back in the mid-'70s, a guy came into your custom paint shop to look at your work with his 11-year-old son?" asked the airbrusher. "He showed you pictures of the boy's work and said that all he wanted to do was draw. He also told you that the boy worshipped all the airbrushers who worked at car shows, custom painting the show cars and vans. 'The boy would be happy to sweep up and clean the shop on weekends or do any odd jobs, just to learn a little bit about airbrushing,' the guy offered. 'You wouldn't even have to pay him.'" (At that time, there were no classes, books, videos, or anything else on the subject of airbrushing. The only way to learn was through self-teaching or by working for a professional.)

The painter at the shop looked at the kid's drawings and leafed through the scrapbook. He tossed the book back to the kid and replied, "The best advice I can give you is to stop wasting your time drawing pictures. There is no room in this industry for any more airbrushers, and I don't have the time to baby-sit you. You'd be wasting my time as well as your own." Feeling a little dejected, the father and son then left.

After hearing the story, the gentleman's wife socked her husband in the arm. "See! I told you not to be so mean to all those kids who used to come by! You deserve this!"

To all the kustom painters out there who never had the time to teach or help out those of us who only wanted to learn, you will be forgotten. This book is dedicated to those of you who helped me and countless others in reaching our goals. Your talents and names will live forever.

Rock on!

Craig Fraser

CHAPTER 1

TO URETHANE OR NOT TO URETHANE?

Before we get to all the fun stuff, we should discuss materials and paint technology. While some people currently use water-based textile paints in helmet and motorcycle painting, I don't recommend it. At present, the automotive painting industry primarily uses automotive paints, so that's what we'll focus on. Although you can apply a number of techniques within this book to water-based paints, if you use them, I can't vouch for their reproduction quality due to lack of durability, colorfastness, and difficulty of application. Eventually, water-based products may be applicable to automotive work, and then I'll gladly eat my words. Until that time, let's use the right tools for the job. (And when water-based paints do

become feasible, just cross this paragraph out. Maybe we should have perforated the page!)

The dictionary defines polyurethane as "any of various polymer or plastic resins of a high molecular weight used in making tough, resistant coatings and adhesives." But, I'm afraid Webster's fell a little short on helping us with this one. For those of you who are isocyanate-challenged, we're talking about automotive paints here. Throughout this century, automotive paints have evolved from lead-based enamels to nitrocellulose lacquers and from synthetic enamels to epoxy, finally evolving into today's polyurethanes. This is not to say that the older paints are extinct; many of them still exist in one form or another. But current technology favors the urethanes.

Modern urethane-based paints are the most visible of the paint families, since the majority of new cars today are painted with them. Categorized as solvent-based polymers, acrylic urethanes and urethane enamels have a higher solids content and a more durable resin base than their distant cousins, the water-based acrylics.

Their catalyzed resins give them more ultraviolet (UV) and oxidation resistance. Also, the higher solids content gives them added durability and a harder shine than the oil-based and synthetic enamels. Although there are water- and ammonia-based urethanes on the market, they don't have the same resin base and aren't suitable for automotive application at this time.

Unlike water-based paints, urethanes do not dry by evaporation, but require instead a catalyzing agent, hardener, or reactive reducer to set chemically. Once set, they're permanent and will not revert to their previous form when exposed to solvents or water. When hardened, they can then be sanded, clear-coated, or even polished to a high shine.

Automotive urethanes are the mainstay of all the major automotive paint companies and are used by the Big Three auto manufacturers as well as many kustom outlets. Names like House of Kolor, Valspar, PPG, and Spies-Hecker, among others, are synonymous with high-quality urethane products. Although these companies may have similar resin bases in their paint products, they're fiercely competitive and often specialize in different fields of painting.

Choosing among urethane products is often a matter of personal preference, though availability also comes into play. If the only distributor in your area carries DuPont, then I guess you're going to use DuPont. It's often that simple. This book is slightly

One of the best ways for airbrush artists to break into hard surface/urethane airbrushing, "The Kustom Helmet." (As long as they don't stray to the dark side and use T-shirt paint.... Sorry, I'll put the soapbox away....)

Polyurethanes offer the best durability, shine, and fuel resistance for the very-picky kustom bike industry.

Next to snowmobiles, the kustom vehicles that get the most abuse are the jet skis. The adhesion and durability of urethane comes through once again.

'Nuff said!

The Craig Fraser House of Kolor urethane airbrush kits available exclusively from Coast Airbrush.

House of Kolor- and Valspar-biased because that's what I use, but you can modify the paint techniques in order to use any of the popular urethanes available today.

If you have multiple suppliers in your area, then consider yourself lucky. I recommend trying the major brands to see which ones fit your budget and style. All the major paint producers that supply urethanes do so in the single-stage and two-stage formats, and sometimes in the three-stage format. Knowing these formats will get you on the right track to urethane addiction.

Single-stage urethane is a combination of inert toners/pigments and urethane clear. It's designed for single color paint jobs where a separate clear coat is not desired. Many budget paint and body shops favor this type of product because it provides instant shine without the need for clearing. Single-stage urethane is easy to apply and is more durable than synthetic or oil-based enamels. But because of its toxicity, slow drying time and isocyanate-based catalysts, it's not a good choice for the airbrush artist.

Two-stage urethanes are characterized primarily as basecoats. They have a dull appearance when sprayed, so it's necessary to clearcoat them to attain a shine and protect the surface. Because of their fast drying time and the large color selection available, including transparent kandies, opaques and pearls, two-stage urethanes are excellent for automotive airbrushing.

Two-stage basecoats use a reactive reducer and/or diluting reducer over an isocyanate-based catalyst for reduction and control of material drying time. Often used for graphics, multi-color paint jobs, and touch-ups, two-stage basecoats are available in smaller quantities at paint stores, making it easier on the airbrush artist's wallet.

Three-stage, or multiple-stage, paints involve an added coat of clear containing a pearl that is sprayed before the final clearcoat. These paints are seen frequently on production cars that have a multiple pearl effect. Though not difficult to apply, they can be a nightmare to repair or match in case of a scratch or collision. Any time an airbrushed effect is added to a graphic, it can be considered a multiple-stage paint application. The Kameleon colors by House of Kolor, and the other holographic paints out there, are in this category, but only because of their need for a black base. These paints actually consist entirely of multisided holographic foils and have no actual pigment or mica pearls. Surprisingly, they are the easiest to repair and touch up, and they cover well. (But they cost a small fortune.)

AIRBRUSHING CONSIDERATIONS

Because of the nozzle size difference between an automotive spray gun and an airbrush, additional reducing and straining may be required when mixing urethanes to prevent clogging in some of the finer airbrushes. Whenever airbrushing with these products, it's a good idea to make sure your airbrush is compatible with such solvent-based paints. Any internal plastic or neoprene parts can become corroded or dissolved by the urethanes and mineral spirits.

Though not as dangerous as catalyzed single-stage paints, two-stage basecoats are still toxic due to their solvents. A good dual-cartridge respirator (a charcoal-based cartridge with pre-filters rated for organic vapors) and proper ventilation are a must when using any form of urethane. Also, try to avoid skin contact with the paints. Different pigments have different toxicity levels and the reducers can dry out your skin. (By the way, pigment toxicity is still an issue in water-based paints as well. Cadmium is still Cadmium, a liver toxin. The difference is that in water it's absorbed into your system more easily. Things that make you go "hmmm....")

Though it's not a urethane, One Shot lettering enamel is a popular choice for pinstriping or lettering on top of automotive urethanes. A single-stage enamel, One Shot dries with a semi-gloss shine and is excellent for striping over a completed paint job. The problems start when you try to clear over it.

If you're going to clear over any enamel, oil-based or synthetic, it's necessary to add a few drops of the same catalyst that is to be used in the final clearcoat. This will prevent the enamel from reactivating and wrinkling, thus ruining your paint job. For those of you who have had this happen, you know what I mean, and you're either smiling or writhing on the floor in agony. Chromatic just came out with a new catalyst that works extremely well for these non-catalyzed enamels. Check it out.

Another option is to use the true urethane striping enamels from House of Kolor/Valspar. They only need to be catalyzed when they're not clearcoated. And they have a completely different selection of colors than One Shot.

WATERBORNE URETHANES

Here's a peek into the future of automotive kustomizing. Waterborne urethanes are new on the market. These coatings have low VOCs (volatile organic compounds). They have good solvent resistance and durability, but they do not have the shine of the solvent-based urethanes. These are 2K systems that need special mixing to incorporate the hardener. After the water evaporates, the two components react with each other and form a tough crossed-linked film, with little or no overspray and very little fumes or solvent emissions.

The only drawback is the need for a climate controlled, dust free spray booth. The long dry time and difficult application make the waterborne urethanes poor candidates for airbrushing. But hey! It's new. Give it a break. If you think this stuff is weird, you should check out some of the funky powder painting systems Valspar and the Chrysler division are experimenting with. Though much of this technology is still on the drawing boards, most likely it's the future of automotive painting. (I can't say the same thing about kustomizing, though!)

Now, I hope I haven't completely confused the majority of you. Although

Replacing lacquers, urethane toners and polyurethane clears are finding a new home in the kustom guitar market.

Who can forget the infamous hood mural? 100% HoK urethane basecoat.

New to the fine art scene, automotive urethanes are being seen more and more in many art galleries. This piece, "Hot Gods and Tiki Rods," was recently sold to a Japanese collector at the CoProNason Tiki-Art show.

A good example of combining airbrushed mural work with kustom graphics. This paint job has been on the road over five years and still looks as if it were just painted.

I like to use Valspar and House of Kolor (HoK) products, if these companies suddenly decided to go into the drapery business, I'm sure I'd get along fine with something else. The important thing is not to get hung up on brand names, but to try as many of the paints on the market as you can. Again, it's important to realize that the techniques described in this book will work with any viable automotive paint. And maybe someday waterbase will be viable. Stranger things have happened in this industry.

I use urethane for my own techniques, as well as those I've developed and borrowed from other artists. Who knows? You might come up with some new style or technique (and then have the joy of staying up until three in the morning writing a book about it).

Even the plastic side moldings on this mini-truck got the airbrush treatment. The mural has lasted longer than the factory treatment that came on these pieces.

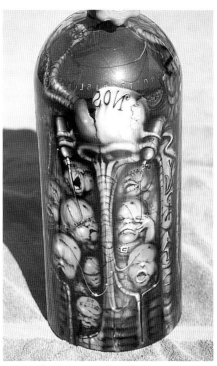

Even the nitrous bottle in a race-car becomes a canvas for a little airbrushing.

A bit of airbrushing and a few caricatures help autograph this House of Kolor sponsored vehicle.

CHAPTER 2

HARD ROCKIN'
"THE GRANITE EFFECT"

Popular with sign painters for years, the "granite" or "stone" effect has had a recent successful run in the mini-trucking and Harley industries. "Granite" serves a dual purpose as a graphic effect and as a neutral backdrop. Its medium gray value coordinates well with any color and acts as a good background canvas for multiple color graphics. Neutral grays and silvers are important as backdrops to many graphic designs, because of their ability to tie in the individual colors without competing with the design itself. (Plus, if used as a bottom graphic on a car or truck, the granite effect successfully hides rock chips.) The effect works well with silvers, by the way, and gives a pretty funky reflective look when done with pearls incorporated into the colors.

For this demo, I used a powder-coated metal sign blank. For practice, use any powder-coated or previously painted metal panel. I highly recommend practicing and experimenting on sign blanks when airbrushing. First, you can clearcoat and keep them as graphic examples; second, it's better for your health than experimenting on a client's car or Harley. (This is known as the 350 lb. Harley Owner Rule; no matter what size respirator you wear, nothing will protect you from this health hazard.)

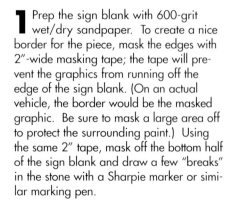

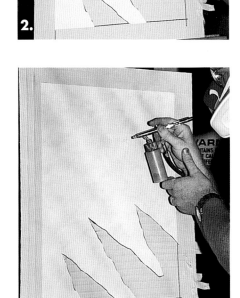

1 Prep the sign blank with 600-grit wet/dry sandpaper. To create a nice border for the piece, mask the edges with 2"-wide masking tape; the tape will prevent the graphics from running off the edge of the sign blank. (On an actual vehicle, the border would be the masked graphic. Be sure to mask a large area off to protect the surrounding paint.) Using the same 2" tape, mask off the bottom half of the sign blank and draw a few "breaks" in the stone with a Sharpie marker or similar marking pen.

2 With an X-Acto knife, cut and peel off the area to be painted, leaving the breaks masked. On a vehicle, take great care when cutting tape so as not to score the surface. This can cause lifting later on when you unmask. A good trick for getting a rough broken surface is to tear the masking tape before laying out the breaks.

3 Using a mixture of black and white urethane basecoat, create a medium gray color with which to base the stone effect. HoK BC 25 and 26 basecoats work well for this, since they bite into the surface of the paint and won't wipe off while working. Using solvent-based urethane is also the best way to prevent reaction problems when clearcoating later. Spray the medium gray onto the surface using an Iwata Eclipse bottom-feed airbrush. To give the stone a natural, uneven appearance, allow the airbrush to streak the surface instead of applying an even coat. Make sure to follow the direction of the breaks to emphasize the grain direction of the stone.

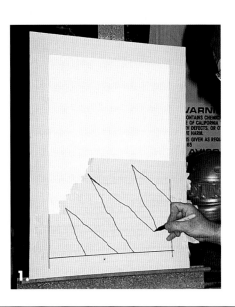

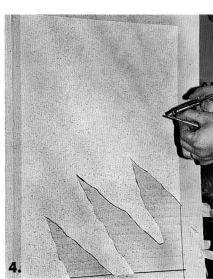

4 Keeping the gray basecoat in the airbrush, I use a little T-shirt airbrush trick I picked up from Terry Hill to give the speckled texture of the stone. Using one-half of a clothes pin, (a popsickle stick works just as well) place the stick under and against the airbrush's tip. When spraying, the paint will now load up on the end of the stick, and flick off giving the speckled effect. When using a larger fan-tipped gun, you can use a piece of cardboard laid over the top to create the same effect.

5 With the entire surface covered in the gray stippling, switch over to black. It's usually a good idea to practice on a sample board, so as not to ruin your actual graphic. By varying the angle of the stick against the tip you can not only vary the quantity of stippling, but vary the size as well. (The more shallow the angle, the finer the stipple, and so on). Be careful at this stage not to get "clothespin-happy" and obliterate your gray; the stone will get dark very fast when spraying black.

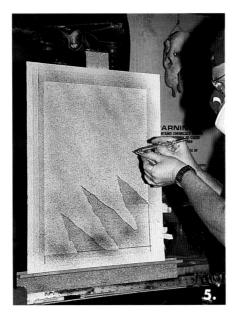

6 Switch to pure white basecoat and apply the final touches to the texture. Not much white is needed to create a good stone effect, so remember the old airbrush rule: Less is more. Again, remember to mask the surrounding area well. This may be a good time to look around your shop to see how many vehicles and clients are starting to take on the appearance of stone. If you can't seem to get the hang of this effect, don't worry. Speckling can also be achieved by other methods. For example, you can lower the air pressure of your brush until it starts to spit. On top-feed models, you can flick the trigger before spraying to load up the needle, thus creating a stipple. And if this doesn't work, don't forget the good ol' toothbrush flick.

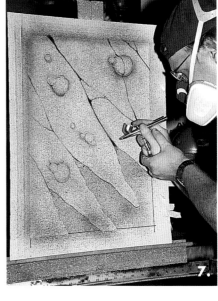

7 When the stippling is finished, airbrush the cracks and inclusions in the stone using a thinned down solution of black urethane and the Iwata HP-C. You can create this weak black by over-reducing your existing black basecoat about 1:1 (1 part paint:1part reducer). Use the weak black to sketch the cracks. If you make a mistake, the transparent black won't cover up the stone's texture. Nothing ruins a good stone effect faster than too much opaque. Keeping everything transparent will also give the effect more depth after you finish the painting and the clearcoat reactivates the basecoats.

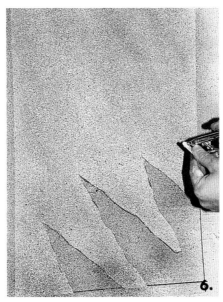

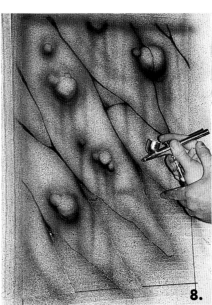

with gravity, for the water streaks. (Just like in nature!) The third element of the stone is the shadows. To oppose grain direction, choose a light source in the upper right (or left) section of the design. Always consider these things before you start painting; you wouldn't want them to conflict with other areas of your paint job.

8 After the sketching is complete, continue layering to darken the cracks and drop shadows. (You can thicken your black solution if you find that it's too watery.) Add water streaks to the surrounding areas of the stone to give them an aged look. Always make sure to paint in the direction of the grain, and

9 Create the broken edge of the stone by using a moveable mask and following it with the airbrush. You can use something ordinary, such as a business card or torn piece of masking tape, to mask the edge. After completing the stone's edge, you can soften it with a little freehand fogging if necessary.

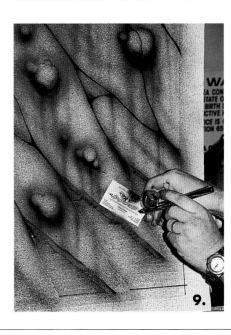

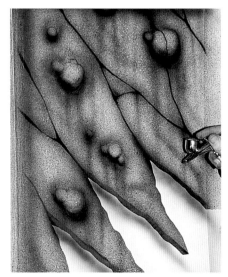
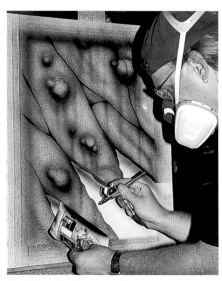
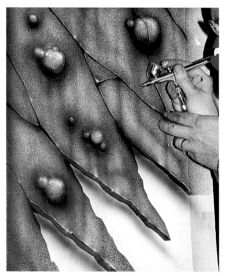

10 When you've finished applying black to the stone's surface, remove the masking of the stone's breaks (being careful not to lift the border). Following the light source, add drop shadows to the lower left of the breaks. This will separate the stone from the background and add a sense of depth.

11 Switching to white and using a freehand shield, spray in a few light reflections across the surface. Again, it's important to keep the white as thin as possible to maintain transparency. Nothing will muddy a surface faster than opaque white.

12 Continue with white to trace the side of the cracks where the light would fall, giving them a very thin high-lighted edge. Also add a few reflections and hot spots off the outcroppings and inclusions. Though the hot spots may not be completely authentic, they create a nice effect and make the stone punch out more.

13 The final step is the clearcoating and buffing. The only drawback is that, because of the stippling, the surface may require a few extra coats of clear before it will flow out. This is also a good reason not to stipple too heavily; it can haunt you later in expensive multiple clearcoats.

MATERIAL & EQUIPMENT

600-grit wet/dry sandpaper
3M 2" masking tape
Clothespin
Sharpie marker or other marking pen
X-Acto knife
House of Kolor (HoK) Basecoat Black Urethane BC-25
HoK Basecoat White Urethane BC-26
HoK Basecoat Reducer RU-311
Iwata HP-C top-feed airbrush
Iwata Eclipse bottle-feed airbrush
Iwata Micron-C

This effect is sure to drum up some "ooohs" and "aaahs" for your graphics (known as the "Oooooh, Aaaaah = $ Factor" by Terry Hill, T-shirt guru and clothespin master). Whether you use this effect for graphics or lettering, the important thing is to experiment. Try different colors, combine the effect with marblizer, etc. The best way to make an effect yours is to modify it with your own style and create something truly unique. While many people in the graphic industry may view the Granite Effect as slightly played out, in the automotive paint industry it always seems to pop back up in popularity. Remember, no effect ever becomes truly outdated; just the painters using them if they don't stay on top of their own game.

Paint On.

CHAPTER 3

MARBLE & MALACHITE
"FAUX FINISHING A MARBLE EFFECT WITH THE AIRBRUSH"

One of the great secrets in coming up with F/X for the graphics industry is to beg, borrow, or steal them from other industries, especially the faux finish industry. As old as the techniques it copies, faux finishing is the re-manufacturing of an appearance without the hassle of using the original building materials. The faux finish used in this chapter is marble.

Whether you use it as a real or faux finish in a home, or as a design element in a graphic scheme, marble has maintained its popularity over the years. Marblizing is so popular in today's industry (borrowed from the funky effects of the `70s), that one trick to individualize it would be to establish a background effect with the textural qualities of actual marble or types of marbled stone. (After all, marblizing or "ragging" effects are cool, but they don't really look like stone, now do they?)

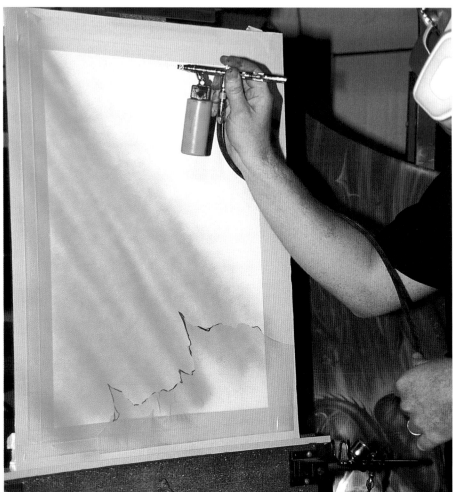

2 With a mixture of HoK (House of Kolor) white basecoat and Kandy Organic Green KBC basecoat, spray in the base color of the marble with an Iwata Eclipse bottom-feed airbrush. In this demo, because I want a textured, grained effect, I'm not as concerned about even coverage of the surface and allow a streaked finish to remain. (Make sure to streak the surface in the same direction as the breaks in the frisket to mimic the natural grain of marble.)

1 Using a red Scotch-Brite pad, scuff the surface of a powder-coated white sign blank and mask the border. To convey the look of a broken edge on the bottom of the marble, cut out a piece of transparent frisket to mask the area. (Always test a small piece of the frisket you're using to be sure it's urethane proof.)

3 To create a more luminescent marble, add a layer of HoK Neutral Marblizer. To color the marblizer, add a combination of turquoise and lazuli blue dry pearl before spraying (you can use other colors of pearl for varied colors of stone). After spraying the entire surface with a good, wet coat, apply a piece of freezer-wrap to the surface and pull away. This gives the surface of the stone a crinkled effect that mimics the mineral variations in many types of marble. Though this step is not necessary to give a good marble effect in the graphic, it does give the finished piece a pretty cool look.

4 Give the marblizer a few minutes to dry, then add a little more texture to the effect with some random stippling and shading, using a darker transparent phthalo green. Use either a clothes pin or a popsicle stick to accomplish this Terry Hill stipple effect (remember the granite effect in Chapter 2). By holding the stick against the edge of the airbrush, the paint builds up on the end and blows off in different-sized specks. The sizes of the specks are determined by the angle of the stick against the nozzle. Be careful not to get too clothespin-happy and stipple the surface too much, or it will look more like granite than marble. (Definitely practice before you try it on your client's Porsche.)

5 After finishing the dark shading and stippling, switch back to HoK basecoat white and add a drop of the Kandy Green toner. This prevents the white from standing out too much. Using this mixture, airbrush in the thin, wispy veins of the marble with a Micron-C detail brush. Maintaining the same general direction for the veins, try to give randomness to the lines by concentrating them in certain focal areas. To add detail in the texture, stipple slightly with this color.

6 Airbrushing within a graphic would normally be enough to create a nice effect. But for those times when nice isn't enough, you can always include the additional detail of a beveled edge. Using standard 3M masking tape, create a secondary border by masking off the desired bevel. Since the bottom edge is broken in this particular marble, the bevel will actually emphasize the distressed marble by showing the stark contrast between the crumbling edge and machined surface.

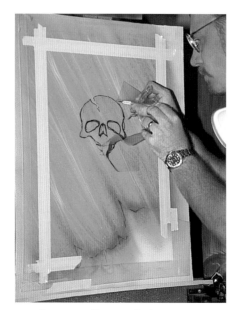

7 If you're still unsatisfied, you can add the classic evil carved skull in the marble effect. (I had to have some fun!) Draw the outline of the skull on a piece of frisket with a Sharpie pen, then cut out the design using an X-Acto knife. Remove the surrounding frisket so a positive stencil remains. Be careful not to press too hard with the knife or you'll score the surface, which can cause etching and lifting problems later on when clearcoating.

8 Fortify and darken the skull by adding a few drops of HoK black basecoat and some HoK Organic Green Kandy Koncentrate. (All of these urethanes are two-stage basecoat urethanes.) This green/black color is used to darken and emphasize the broken edge and the shadows cast by the carved skull. It's a good idea to fog a light coat of this color around the taped and masked areas—just enough to contrast with the masked areas without obliterating all of the textured work underneath.

9 Remove the tape, noting how just a slight contrast in value can give the illusion of a machined edge. To emphasize the machined corners, use an Artool freehand shield to temporarily mask the diagonal bevel. Though you can use masking tape, shields are good because of the speed involved, and you can use them even when the paint is still too fresh to mask.

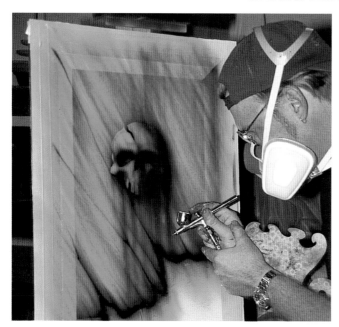

10 Remove the frisket from the skull area. Airbrush the details and soften the masked edges using the same dark transparent phthalo green. Add water streaks and any touchups to the machined edge, using the freehand shield. Whenever spraying with urethanes, or any other paint for that matter, it's important to have good ventilation and a good respirator. A dual-cartridge respirator traps all airborne paint fumes and dust.

11 Airbrush the fine highlights and finishing hot spots using the white/green mixture. For white highlights, less is more. Although highlights can make a piece, they can also obliterate your previous details. To prevent this, try thinning the white until it's transparent. Using this thinned solution and the freehand shield, re-emphasize the beveled edge and skull to give the illusion of an upper left light source.

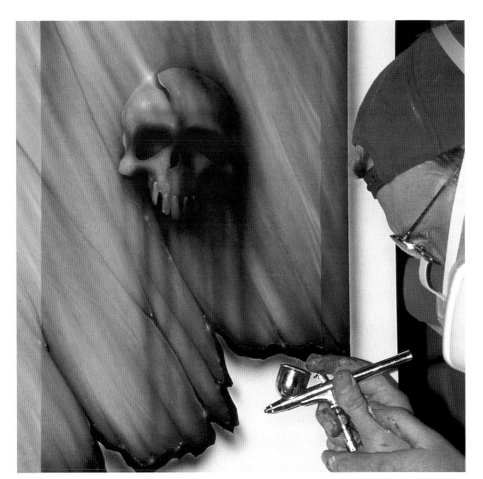

MATERIAL & EQUIPMENT

3M red Scotch-Brite pad
3M masking tape
Solvent-proof frisket (or transparent transfer tape)
X-Acto knife
Artool FH-1 Freehand Shield
House of Kolor (HoK) Basecoat White Urethane BC-26
HoK Kandy Organic Green, KBC-9
HoK Basecoat Black BC-25
HoK Transparent /Neutral Marblizer MB-00
HoK Lazuli Blue/Turquoise dry pearl
HoK Reducer RU-311
Plastic wrap
Iwata HP-C top-feed airbrush
Iwata Eclipse bottle-feed
Iwata Micron-C

12 Remove all the masking. For a 3-D effect, use a weak black toner to give the finished piece a nice drop shadow for the broken edges of the marble. (The only step left is conning K-Daddy into shooting it with some clearcoat.)

13 Since two-stage urethane basecoats dry to a dull finish, they require a catalyzed clear not only to protect the surface, but also to bring out the pearls and give the finished kandy colors that "reach-into-it-with-your-arm" shine and depth. At Kal Koncepts, we tell people that there are really three stages of completion to our paint jobs: a) The paintwork and graphics; b) The airbrushing, pinstriping, and drop shadows; and c) The clearcoated finished product. (The most notable of the three, the clearcoat, brings the paint job to life. Let's face it, without clear, paint jobs are plain boring.)

This effect, or faux finish, is a nice break from the norm when airbrushing fades and drop shadows. I especially like using a silver-based marble effect in the background of my graphics. A neutral silver allows the graphics to play off one another without competing with the background or base color of the vehicle. (Plus, it gives me a nice area on which to drop-shadow graphics when I'm working on a black car!)

Keep on Marblizing!

CHAPTER 4

EARTH, WOOD, & FIRE

"CREATIN' A WOODIE WITHOUT WOOD."

A long-time faux finish, but recent arrival into kustom automotive airbrushing, is the wood grain technique. The first time I used this technique was to create a wood paneled effect on a Fatboy Harley; but I found that the wood effect was also a nice touch when applied with other graphics or as a neutral background. This effect is a classic texture dating back to the old "Woodie" car designs of the 1940s-'50s. It's one of the few effects that is equally enjoyed by multiple generations and multiple automotive cultures.

1 Mask a sign blank, single-staged black. Using HoK Basecoat White, (It's not necessary to have a black base for the wood, but since it is most difficult to build a light colored demo on a dark surface, I suggest learning it this way) with a vertical streaking action, spray a repeating pattern of dagger strokes to mimic the texture of woodgrain. To create a knothole, contour the streaks to blend in with the knothole itself, much as it would appear in real wood grain.

2 Don't use the white for the actual coloring of the piece, but as a base to build the colors on. (Often, when painting a woodie effect on a vehicle, you don't have the luxury of beginning over a white base; by using the underlying color as a background, the wood will have a natural tie-in with the color of the vehicle.) Whenever working on a dark surface with transparent kandy toners, such as HoK, it's necessary to give a light-colored base to play off. Otherwise, you're not going to see the colors very well. Airbrush in the vertical woodgrain streaks, continuing the line off the board and onto the taped area. This gives the wood a continuous look and prevents the appearance of the actual return stroke.

3 When you've completed the white base value, use HoK SG-101 Lemon Yellow to begin layering in the base color of the wood. It's important not to go back over the same line work as the white, but merely to accent it. Since the colors are semi-transparent, this varied layering will give the wood an added depth. Little, if any, of the white should remain in the yellowed area; again, the white is merely a tool to define and base the colors.

4 Switch to your HP-C for finer detailing and also switch colors to a more transparent red oxide. You can create this color by combining Tangerine Kandy, a few drops of Root Beer, Pagan Gold Kandy Koncentrate, and intercoat clear. As you build up colors and progress in the layering, decrease the amount of work you do on the surface. Don't cover all the yellow with the red oxide color. Leave some to show through to give the piece depth and texture. Try getting into the habit of wiping down your surface with a soft lint-free towel or cloth diaper, moistened with a little water and pre-cleaner. This will prevent the overspray from building up and the wet surface will give you an idea of how it's going to look when clearcoated.

5 It takes two passes to give the design an even coverage that's not too splotchy, yet not too dark. It's better to build lightly in layers than to try to save time with one heavy coat. The time spent in building up the gradual colors and detail more than pays off in the quality of the finished piece. (It's also easier to correct mistakes while building layers, rather than go back and repaint the entire area).

6 Mix Violette Kandy with a little red oxide mixture and a few drops of BC-25 Black. Begin accenting and emphasizing the knothole areas and some of the primary grain patterns. Don't cover the entire area with the violet/black; just a few places to break up the color. You can also try a trick called "pulling" or (as it actually appears) "smearing." Wet an area with the airbrush, then streak the paint with your finger or a rag and pull it down to its initial basecoat to give the wood a realistic, burned effect. Never use lacquer thinner for this effect. While it may appear to work, it can also cause irreparable damage to the underlying basecoat and could cause lifting.

8 For a finishing touch, you can paint a few "nails" in the wood. This is especially effective when creating a faux wood paneling and is a good stylized way of rendering wood. To create the nails, bring the airbrush closer than you normally would when airbrushing a dot. The term for this technique is a "blowout" and it's a good example of how to turn an airbrushing disadvantage into a kustom effect. If you decide to get a little carried away, the way I did, you can add some half-circles around the nails to give the illusion of the hammer hitting the wood as the nails were pounded in.

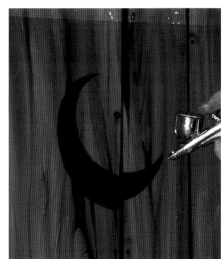

7 When the wood graining is finished, add a little more black to the violet/black mixture and add a few seams and breaks in the wood. Use two strips of 3/4" tape approximately 1/6" to 1/8" apart to spray the crisp edges of the individual boards. Normally, I would caution about having any overspray go over your tape edge, but with all this wood grain you'd probably never notice it. (Heck...it might even look better.)

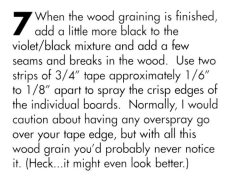

9 It's always fun to take a design one step further than originally planned. When I created this design, the wood reminded me of an old outhouse door. (What can I say? I was inspired.) Using some of the black/violet mixture left in my gun, I proceeded to airbrush the classic moon-shaped door vent. You can either sketch it out first or just start spraying. The best thing about this type of design is that any imperfections in the linework will just look like imperfections in the wood.

10 Unlike flames, fire is easy to create because it can be completely random. Much like the technique used to create the wood grain, you can create sweeping dagger strokes to mimic the licks of an actual flame. But with fire, you can cross over the lines a bit if you want to. Imagine a grouping of dagger strokes, starting out thick at the base and then all tapering to points.

11 To give the fire an eerie effect, use a Skullmaster "Multiple" template to fog in some little ghost faces (K-Daddy calls them "screamy faces.") throughout the flame. This is a nice automotive touch, since you can only see the images up close. If you're riding or just walking by, they blend in and look like part of the fire.

12 Layer over the white using the same yellow basecoat. To give the fire more realism, add a few small patches clinging from the edges of the boards. (Yes, that is an eye peeking out of the vent hole. After all, it wouldn't be an outhouse fire without a victim!)

13 Don't use the Tangerine Kandy to completely cover the yellow of the fire. Instead, just color in the tips of the flames. A lot of yellow should show through, not just to make the fire look more realistic, and hotter, but also to contrast with the darkness of the background.

14 Also use the Tangerine to give color to the retina of the eye and to emphasize the shapes of the faces in the flames. Without the airbrushing on the faces, they would retain a crisp-edged stenciled look. By adding just a bit of airbrush to the shadows, you soften the edges and the entire piece appears to have been done freehand.

15 Switch brushes to a .2 mm HP-C. Because of the need for pinpoint detail in the highlighted edges and burning embers, this detail gun is necessary. It also does a good job of atomizing the white for the smoke. Go back to the black/violet mixture to paint the pupils and eye details. Then, switch to an over-reduced mixture of white for the highlights and hot base of the fire.

A little wood paneling was airbrushed in this truck bed to accent the stereo installation.

MATERIAL & EQUIPMENT

3M masking tape
X-Aacto knife
House of Kolor (HoK)
Basecoat White Urethane
BC-26
HoK Basecoat Black
Urethane BC-25
HoK Lemon Yellow SG-
101
HoK Intercoat Clear SG-
100
HoK Tangerine Kandy
Koncentrate KK-8
HoK Root Beer Kandy
Koncentrate KK-7
HoK Pagan Gold Kandy
Koncentrate KK-12
HoK Violette Kandy
Koncetrate KK-17
HoK Reducer RU-311
Iwata HP-C top-feed
airbrush
Iwata HP-CS Eclipse
top-feed airbrush

16 Scratching is another technique that you can use to accent the edge of the wood and eliminate the possibility of overspray. This trick is primarily used in illustration, but if done carefully, it can give very nice effects in automotive, too. When using the scratching technique, always use a sharp blade, and be careful not to score the paint. Otherwise, you can have lifting and paint-peeling problems.

17 And there you have it—one wood-paneled piece ready for clearcoat. While you don't need to turn yours into an outhouse, set it on fire, or have someone trapped inside, these fun little options show how easy it is, and how many ways there are, to modify a simple wood grain demo into a design in progress. And it's nice to have these little tricks under your belt when you need them.

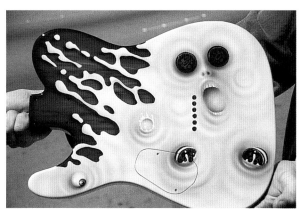

The wood grain effect as the background adds a nice retro woodie touch to this otherwise radical overkill graphic job.

Even this guitar received a little wood grain treatment under the graphics. (Especially handy when the original wood grain has been too damaged to re-clear.)

Now go play with your wood.

CHAPTER 5

RIPPED TO SHREDS

"HAVIN' A LITTLE FUN WITH RIPPED METAL AND BRAINS"

Continuing with the faux effects theme, I've just got to throw in a little metal effects demo. And where you have metal, you have rips, tears, and exposed brains in the background, of course. (Hey, it's my demo, I get to do what I like.). Actually, it's a good way to combine effects, and rendering brains is a good way to practice negative/positive space drawing techniques.

1 Prepare the sign blank with 600–grit sandpaper and spray the entire surface with a medium-grade silver basecoat. Before picking up the airbrush, it's a good idea to sketch out the ripped area in chalk. This will help center the image and, in more complicated designs, will serve as a massing study. Chalk is a better sketching tool than pencil, since it's easily removed from the surface and is inert, unlike Stabilo, or other grease-based pencils.

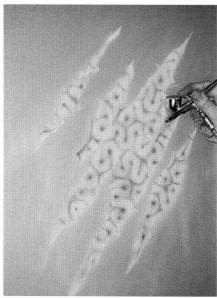

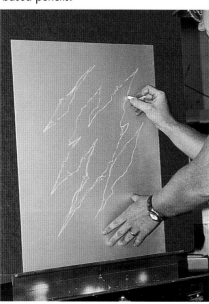

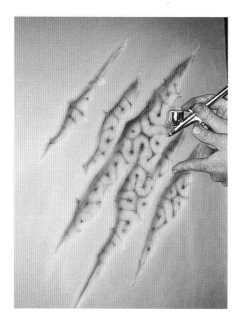

2 Airbrush the sketched area with SG-102 Chromium Yellow. The yellow acts as a base for the "brain" effect behind the torn metal. Though I prefer to freehand the background on small projects, you can use frisket or masking tape on larger designs to prevent overspray problems. Before going on to the next color, wipe the surface down with a precleaner. Besides eliminating oils and contaminants, the precleaner removes any overspray from the surrounding silver area that may be locked down by later airbrushing.

3 Mix equal parts of HoK Tangerine and Root Beer KBC Kandy basecoats to create a transparent red oxide toner. (You can also add intercoat clear to this mixture to increase the transparency and improve the flow characteristics.) Lightly sketch the outline of the brain tissue. This is tricky because you have to deal with the design in the negative form by drawing the seams between the folds. It's important to keep the spacing equal between the folds, or it will lose its pattern and won't look like a brain.

4 With the red oxide kandy, darken the design and include a drop shadow under the top edge of the rips to increase the sense of depth. The best characteristic of a true kandy is that you can continue to layer with the same color. And, unlike an opaque that will eventually reach its primary hue, the transparent kandy will continue to darken until almost black, but will retain the depth of a transparent. If you're using frisket to mask the area, this would be a good time to remove it. The overspray of the red oxide on the surrounding area will add to the illusion of distressed metal.

MATERIAL & EQUIPMENT

600–grit sandpaper
House of Kolor (HoK) Basecoat Urethane Orion Silver
HoK Black Basecoat BC-25
HoK White Basecoat BC-26
HoK Lemon Yellow Basecoat SG-101
HoK Kandy Tangerine Koncentrate KK-8
HoK Kandy Root Beer Koncentrate KK-7
HoK Kandy Violette Koncentrate KK-17
HoK Kandy Oriental Blue Koncenrtate KK-4
HoK Intercoat Clear SG-100
Iwata HP-C airbrush
Iwata Micron C airbrush

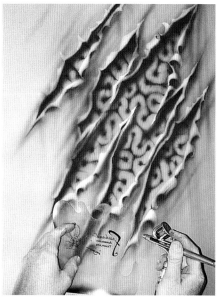

5 Using opaque white and .2 mm Iwata HP-C, begin sketching the ripped curls of the metal. Note that the previously made notches in the yellow areas are the starting points for the rips. At this stage, you'll have to work very closely to the surface to reduce overspray and be very precise with the airbrush. I suggest using a detail brush here, instead of masking. This eliminates the sharp, raised edge that normally results from masking.

6 Create a phthalo blue by combining equal parts HoK Oriental Blue and Cobalt Blue KBC Kandy. Fog in the top of the metal rip on the silver side. It's important to keep the blue overspray away from the yellow area, otherwise you'll end up with a green color due to the transparent nature of the toners. Use the blue to create water streaks and discoloration effects in the metal surface.

7 Switch to the .2-mm detail gun and go back over the brain details with deep violet toner. The violet becomes a reddish brown when sprayed over yellow. The violet also helps continue the discolorations in the metal surface and to shadow the underside rips. To protect the white edge of the rip from overspray, use one of Artool's Freehand Shields while darkening in the drop shadow.

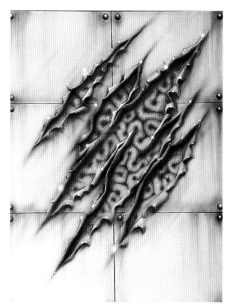

8 To punch out the details, stay with the fine-line airbrush, using a weakened solution of black. It's important not to overdo the black; although a necessary ingredient in this design, too much black can deaden or even kill the depth.

9 Returning to opaque white, use the Artool shield with the Iwata Micron-C to outline the edges of the rips and to put in the hot spots. With a random squiggling motion, lightly add the highlights on the brains to give them a wet look. You must keep the white over-reduced and transparent at this stage, or the overspray will decimate the underlying detail.

10 You can finish the design either by adding some seams and rivets to the background, as I did, or by just leaving it plain, as brain-ridden metal. It's all up to your own sick imaginations!

Later Sprayz!

CHAPTER 6

GETTIN' GRAPHIC

One of the most important yet underrated aspects of automotive painting and kustom graphics is the masking and design set-up. After all, what kind of finished product would we have without the initial design and layout steps? As painters, we tend to get so caught up with the product that we forget to analyze and refine the process. This type of analysis is important to eliminate stagnation, especially in this industry where taste and style change yearly. Since all of my previous tech articles have leaned toward the actual painting and completion of jobs, I thought it would be fun to take a break and look at the design and layout aspects of kustom graphics. Every now and then, it's important to put aside the airbrush candy and focus on building a foundation. So, let's step back and take a look at what we're doing out there anyway.

Unlike the fickle changes in style and graphic design trends, the basic concept of masking has not changed much throughout the years. Its primary focus has always been merely a means to an end: the kustom paint job. While the materials may improve, the intent remains the same: to protect the masked areas from overspray and paint bleed. Now just because I've reduced the masking system down to two steps doesn't mean that there is no art to it. I'm not trying to convince all of you that there is some type of Zen to pulling a piece of masking tape; the art is rather in how you lay it down. Since he's always readily available, I'll use my partner Kyle "K-Daddy" Gann as an example.

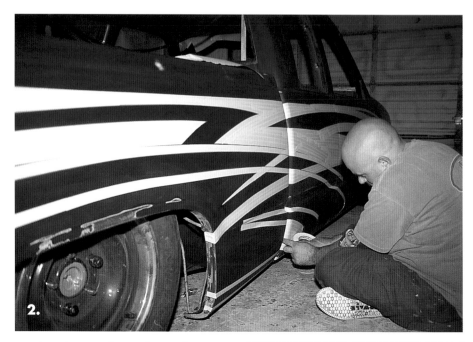

2.

1.

1 Though I may design the graphics in the concept rendering, Kyle is the true genius of the layout. Not only can he lay out the designs in tape faster than I can draw them, but he can also make the changes that are frequently needed when transferring a two-dimensional drawing to a three-dimensional reality.

3.

2-3 When both "K" and Dion work together on a project, the papering, masking, and painting definitely become an art form. With "K" using 1/8" blue vinyl tape for the layout and 3/4" tape for the follow-through, Dion follows with the paper machine and fills in all the exposed areas. The accuracy of the design layout has little to do with actual measurement, but more with referencing key points on the vehicle (wheel, insignia, door handle, etc.). Keeping the paper flat eliminates paint reflection and overspray onto surrounding areas. A wrinkle in the paper can often redirect paint to an unwanted part of the vehicle faster than you can shake a paint stick. Little details like this are what make monumental differences in the final appearance and completion time of any paint project.

While masking tape and paper are the primary tools for our layouts, often a specific design will require something different. A good example is the compound-curved surface of a motorcycle fender or helmet.

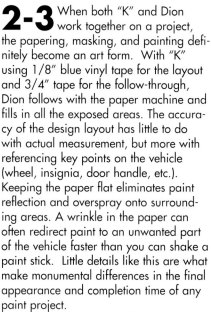

4.

4 On these motorcycle parts, for instance, it was necessary to sketch out the chain links before cutting. Also, the masking system had to be transparent enough to be able to see through to the underlying design. Gerber transfer tape worked perfectly. The adhesion is low enough not to lift the base color, but still strong enough to prevent paint bleed. Another good answer to this problem would have been to use a liquid latex masking system, such as HoK's fluid mask. The only drawback to using a spray mask for this job was that the deadline would not have allowed for the mask to dry.

5 A fairly new tool in today's airbrushing and effects painting is the moveable mask. By using an acetate or photopaper mask, you can reposition the shield to get clean soft edges without tape-lifting or buildup. The one in the photo is a Freehand Shield produced by Artool. The Freehand Shield system allows the freehand airbrusher to accomplish the structure of a technical layout without all the masking and cutting. While these masking systems may seem too simplistic to discuss, it's important to realize that artists cannot excel in what they do until they master the tools of layout. Much like the airbrush. If use of the tool does not become automatic, the result will take on a mechanical look. Remember the Zen of layout: No amount of good spraying or airbrushing can make up for bad preparation.

6 In today's kustom market, the graphics are at a crossroads of sorts. The radical West Coast style of the `90s is dangerously close to becoming overkill-clutter, while the increased popularity of "retro" or "Ol' School" graphics is becoming a parody of its own style. (I'm just making an observation on the growing trends, not a judgment on the styles themselves.) For the clients following a trend, it's an easy choice; they simply point to their favorite paint job in their favorite magazine, and the painter does the rest. What's tricky is coming up with something original. Again, the client just tells the painter he wants something that is unique, edgy, hip, trick, neato, swell, etc. It's basically left in the painter's hands. Every kustom painter then has the choice of imitating or innovating; neither choice is right or wrong. The balance between the two is where the art form lies.

If you look through some older automotive mags, you're sure to see some paint jobs that'll turn your stomach. It's important to realize, though, that they're not necessarily hideous, just being viewed out of their historical and cultural context. Many of the techniques that have returned from the seventies have been modified to fit within the current graphics trend. The trick to developing something timeless is to look at what has remained timeless and what keeps on returning. Reverse engineer the styles themselves until you figure out the common thread among the popular ones. Once you figure this out, you can create designs less destined to become obsolete.

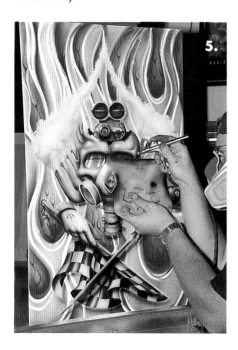

5.

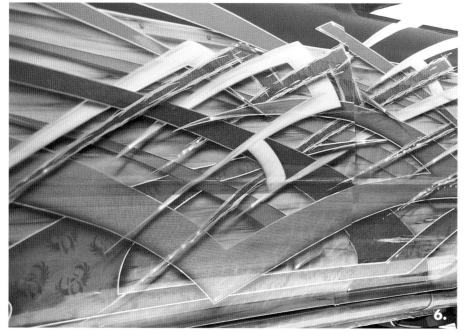

6.

7 A good example of "Ol' School": the classic lines of Larry Watson's Scallop designs of the 1950s and 60s as seen on this 1961 Buick Le Sabre. A bad example is an AMC Pacer (though, it's so ugly that it's almost hip).

7.

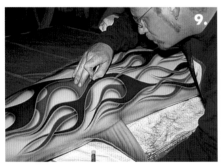

8-9 A good example of a design that never died is the immortal flame job, made into legend by Von Dutch and the living legend Von Franco.

10 Shown here next to his primered and flamed Studebaker truck, Franco's flame job is a perfect example of a classic design incorporated onto a classic ride. Flames are not only not for every person, but definitely not for every vehicle. Graphics and designs must be custom tailored to the personality of both man and machine.

A good trick to analyzing a design on a vehicle, or anywhere else, is to see how it treats the negative space—the area surrounding the design. Architects consider this when designing a home to fit within its environment. The same holds true for graphics on a car. How do the graphics treat the vehicle's natural bodylines? Do the elements and colors contrast with or compliment the existing design? All these factors must be considered for the design to work.

11 Notice how the graphics of this street rod follow the bodylines in a complimentary linear format. The design has the classic rod look recognized as an industry standard among today's great rod and truck painters, such as Santini and Bernt. But like many styles, this classic look existed in the radical paint schemes of the racecars and dragboats of Dick Vale and Bill Carter throughout the 1970s and '80s.

Even the tribal/slash images of the `90s "West Coast" style will eventually seem conservative to some. Graphics won't necessarily become busier, just different. Trends in graphics are often connected to clothing and tattoo designs. The kustom paint job is in many cases merely an extension of the owner's personality. Keeping this in mind, you can often predict future graphics trends by following fashion trends and performing your own interpretation of the style. But be careful not to interpret too literally; not everyone wants a tattoo or tribal pattern on his car. Synthesis of style is what defines the true kustom painters from the mimics.

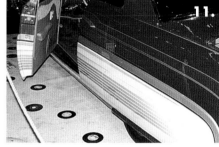

12 Jason Whitfield's green Honda CRX is a hybrid interpretation. Keeping the "West Coast" style that Jason wanted, we also were able to incorporate a biomechanical background with a number of `70s style graphic textures airbrushed throughout. The result is recognizable as the Kal Koncepts style, yet still stands out as unique.

12.

13 Another hybrid style can be seen in Ed "Big Daddy" Roth's Beatnik Bandit II with the reintroduction of the `60s Roth creation. The paintjob was a combination of modern techno-abstract with a caricature of Rat Fink in the graphics.

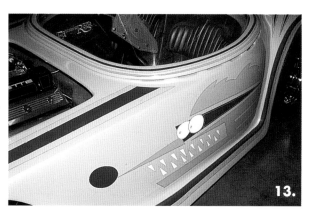

13.

15.

14 Even a simple two-tone can be hyped up by adding a little tribal patterning to it. This proves that radical and conservative styles can work well together to create an altogether different design element. The most common synthesizing of styles happens naturally when you work directly with other artists.

14.

15 Besides lending his incredible pinstriping ability to our shop, Ron Beam of Beam Bros. Racing fame also adds his own style to our graphic designs, giving our look a special edge. This synthesizing of style, whether accidental or deliberate, is what will determine the future of the kustom industry, just as it has earmarked its past.

The painter has an awesome responsibility to determine the direction of his own industry. Every guy out there with a spray gun and a little paint has an equal opportunity to start the newest trend-setting look. Not every field of work has this kind of possibility for self-promotion. Remember the adage, "I may not know much about art, but I know what I like"? This is the client in a nutshell. He or she doesn't know what is going to be the leading trend, but they help determine it. If they won't buy it, we can't sell it.

Paint to live, live to paint.

CHAPTER 7

A DODGE OF A DIFFERENT KOLOR

Las Vegas hosts an annual event that has become the Mecca of the automotive kustomizing and after-market industry. Yes, true believers, I'm talking about the SEMA show. If a company sells after-market parts, paint, rims, or go-fast goodies, you'll find them there. I counted at least one hundred rim companies, and, closer to our hearts, well over a hundred kustom vehicles of every make and model. Not to be left out, the paint companies are there in full force as well. And where there are paint companies there are usually paint jobs on display.

That's where Kal Koncepts got involved. We got our hands on a brand new '97 Dodge Magnum standard cab. With all the accessory companies scrambling for the new Dodge market, what better vehicle to kustomize for the SEMA show? After a few phone calls to our buddies at Borla Exhaust, Bell Tech Suspensions, Gaylord Hardtarps, Colorado Custom Wheels, and Continental Tire, not to mention Jon Kosmoski from House of Kolor, we had ourselves a sponsored vehicle for the show.

Since Kal Koncepts/Air Syndicate's sponsorship involved the most visual part of the vehicle, the paint job, we sat down and worked out a number of designs before sending out color renderings of our Koncept Dodge to all the parties involved. With approval all around, we gave our Christmas list of kandies, pearls, and clearcoats to Jon Kosmoski and waited for the UPS man. You may recall that this truck was featured in *Sport Truck* magazine and the paint job was featured in the now defunct *Autographics* magazine. This is one of the best examples of "West Coast" graphics for which Kal Koncepts has become known. As for a radical version of "West Coast" graphics, don't worry, we'll get to that later in the book.

1 Though fully loaded from the dealer, the truck looked pretty plain when Tony dropped it off. Before we started any paintwork, the truck was lowered by Performance Accessories of Bakersfield, California, with some help from one of the truck's primary sponsors, Bell Tech. Since the SEMA show has always been the showcase for the latest after-market products, we wound up being the guinea pig for the Dodge prototype lowering set-up. Luckily, after the 5" to 7" drop, the only thing that hit the ground was the gas tank, which was promptly relocated.

2 The best thing about new trucks, or any new vehicle for that matter, is that they require little, if any, body work. Still, in order to give a cleaner appearance, the antenna was shaved along with the stake-holes, molding, emblems, and the rear tail-gate handle, which was relocated to the inside of the bed. K-Daddy wet-sanded the entire body with 600-grit sandpaper and then wiped down the entire surface with HoK KC-20 post sanding cleaner in preparation for the graphics. Note the change in stance from the 17" Colorado Custom "Hancock" wheels and the low profile Continental Tires both of which were corporate sponsors for this truck at SEMA.

3 With the truck all prepped and ready, K-Daddy laid out the primary graphic with 1/8" blue vinyl tape. The blue vinyl tape is superior to masking tape due to its resistance to bleeding and its re-positionability in case you make mistakes. (K-Daddy doesn't make mistakes, he just changes his mind.) In this design the primary graphic is a dividing line between the top color of the truck and the lower graphic. This unique style is a key part of most Kal Koncepts paint jobs–it takes the primary color of the car and turns it into a graphic.

4 Because of its "unusual" Metallic Kiwi color (a kind word, we really didn't like the color), we decided to retain a large section of it as a background for the graphics. (Ok, so I had ulterior motives. I actually won a bet that I couldn't use this color in a kustom graphic job.) After masking off the bottom section where the graphics would be placed, K-Daddy gave the Dodge a new look, hitting the top half with some HoK Black. Black not only made the vehicle look smaller and lower, but gave it a nice two-tone contrast to the rest of the paint job.

5 Since the black is a basecoat, it was hit with a light coat of clear. After allowing it to set up overnight, K-Daddy began laying out the first color. Since the graphics were going through the door-jambs, we cut the blue tape at the door edge and wrapped it inside. Though this may sound like an insignificant step, you can ask any kustom painter how much fun it is to watch hours of design work rip off when you accidentally open the door before cutting the tape!

6 After laying tracing paper against the blue tape layout, K-Daddy traced the graphics with a Sharpie pen. Later he would perforate the design with a pounce wheel and chalk it onto the other side of the truck with a pounce bag (a bag of chalk dust used for marking). This old signpainter's trick is a lot easier than running back and forth with a measuring tape to make sure that your lines are all even and exactly the same.

7 After we laid the blue tape over the chalked lines and masked off the first main graphic, the truck went back to the spray booth for a good coat of HoK SG-101 Lemon Yellow Basecoat. K-Daddy made sure the rims were covered to protect them from overspray. With the booth running full blast, the rest of the truck was not fully masked, since the graphics were only in a small area.

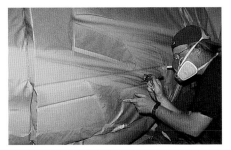

8 Giving the yellow about half an hour to set, I used my Iwata HP-C airbrush to spray in fades and effects. To create a red oxide kandy, I mixed an equal amount of HoK Tangerine Kandy Koncentrate and Root Beer Kandy. The red oxide color gives the yellow a streaked, almost flame-like appearance. A touch of lavender pearl in the mix gives the fire effect a magenta glow when viewed at the right angle.

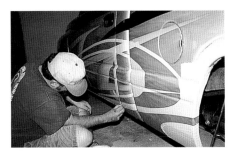

9 For the next graphic, K-Daddy had to work in and around the previous yellow design. This is called wrapping the graphics. To create a 3-D weaving effect, we unmasked certain areas of the yellow while sanding the rest of the exposed underlying graphic smooth to prevent an edge from appearing in the next color.

10 Loading the HVLP (High Volume Low Pressure) spraygun with HoK Tru-Blue Shimrin, K-Daddy sprayed the graphic, beginning with light-tack coats and ending with an even wet coat. Although it takes multiple layers to get the color to lay evenly, too much can give a nasty paint edge that can cost a couple of expensive clearcoats to bury. Because the graphic has an airbrushed effect in it, it wasn't necessary to build up good coverage.

11 I sprayed a water-reflection effect in the blue using white basecoat. This effect resembles the reflections that you see on the bottom of a pool of water. Since I was working with an opaque white, I worked quickly and with an over-reduced solution to eliminate overspray problems.

12 Coming back with a Kandy Oriental blue, I toned the white down and increased the depth of the water reflection. I wasn't worried about the overspray. If anything, I would use it to color and tint the reflection. "One man's overspray is another man's gradated fade."

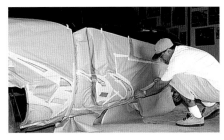

13 Tape down any loose ends or folds in the paper. (These folds can reflect overspray and cause dry areas in the graphic.)

14 Since the next graphic was going to be a series of kandies, K-Daddy first had to spray the area white to give the color a base. To save time, he also masked off and sprayed the area that was going to be the checkerboard. K-daddy is known for spraying more than one graphic at a time. This is how he can apply more than four colors a day on a graphic job.

15 Masking off the boomerang graphics, K-Daddy laid out a grid of 1½" masking tape where the checkerboard was going to be. Cutting and removing every other checker, he sprayed the checkered mask with basecoat black to complete the effect.

16 Giving the black checkers about 15 minutes to dry, K-Daddy taped the upper mask and folded it down over the checkerboard, uncovering the boomerangs to be painted. This quick trick allowed him to quickly begin spraying without having to re-mask. Another time saver was the spectrum fade he was spraying, starting from magenta and working toward violet. By working along the spectrum from light to dark, you can continue adding colors to the gun without having to thoroughly clean it out.

17 Before K-Daddy got too carried away and unmasked everything, I added a violet fade to the checkerboard graphic. (I do this quite often. I can't stand seeing a graphic just sitting there without a fade, plus I like violet). Then, I added a bit of blue/pink interference pearl to give the fade a little kick. Now it had a subtle color shift from purple to magenta, depending on the viewing angle.

18 K-Daddy's favorite part, the background masking (he really hates it). All of the graphics were masked off so the background could be shot and all of the drop shadows airbrushed in. To give you an idea of the amount of masking there is in a complete graphics job, this Dodge required over two miles of 3/4" tape. Honest!

19 Regarding my Kiwi metallic bet, I really didn't like the color and decided to kick it up a notch with some HoK marblizer. A blend of blue/green, turquoise, and lime dry pearl created a multiple hue effect that was then sprayed on using my Iwata RG-2 mini-gun. While the marblizer was still wet, I streaked my fingers through the surface in the direction of the graphics to give the image an illusion of speed. A piece of freezer wrap was also used to give an added marbled effect.

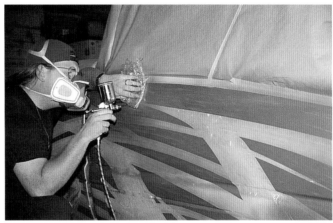

20 After allowing the marblizer to dry, I came back with my airbrush and added flecks and streaks of highly transparent Kandy Organic Green HoK toner. This darkened and toned up the original kiwi background, making it much more vibrant. Transparent white with a small amount of green pearl was also used to add hair-thin veins to the marbled color. All of these transparent layers worked together to give the illusion of depth, much like a translucent stone.

21 To add to the depth of the graphics and create the 3-D illusion, drop shadows were airbrushed in with a weakened solution of black urethane basecoat. This transparent black let the green color of the background through to give a realistic shadow effect.

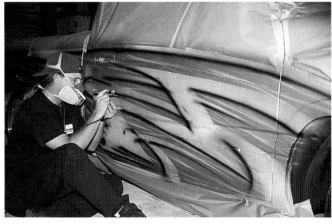

22 After giving the entire truck a light coat of clear and colorsanding, it was time for the pinstriping. Ron Beam was brought in to work his magic on the graphics. Using complimentary and contrasting colors, Ron gave the design his final touch and hid a few questionable edges (and mysterious mistakes made during the design process).

23 Using his trusty Iwata LPH-95 HVLP clearcoat gun, Dion "D-Bob" Giuliano added the series of tack and wet coats of HoK UFC-40 Komply Klear that would make up the final clearcoat. There would be one more clearcoating session to eliminate any graphic edges before the truck was colorsanded and buffed.

24 While it bears little resemblance to the original stock truck, the finished product is still definitely a Dodge. (The boyz at Dodge are breathing a sign of relief.) This entire job took a little more than three weeks (including shipping it all over the state to have all the sponsored goodies fit to it.) Some of the last minute accessories on the front are the molded-in billet grill from Trenz Manufacturing and the smoothy front bumper cover from Traders. A little window tint, a little wax, and we're ready to roll...on to the next job.

Long live trade shows!

MATERIALS & EQUIPMENT

1/8 " 3M blue fineline vinyl tape
3/4" 3M masking tape
36" 3M masking paper
36" tracing paper
Pounce wheel and chalk bag
House of Kolor (HoK) Black Basecoat Urethane BC-25
HoK White Basecoat Urethane BC-26
HoK Lemon Yellow Basecoat SG-101
HoK Tangerine Kandy Koncentrate KK-8
HoK Root Beer Kandy Koncentrate KK-7
HoK Tru Blue Shimrin Basecoat PBC-36
HoK Kandy Oriental Blue Koncentrate KK-4
HoK Intercoat Clear SG-100
HoK Neutral Marblizer MB-00
HoK "a whole mess of green, and blue toned pearls!!!"
HoK Magenta Kandy KBC-1
HoK Striping urethanes
Iwata HP-C top-feed airbrush
Iwata LPH-95 HVLP spraygun
Xcaliber OOO Sword striping brush

CHAPTER 8

FLAMIN'

Since the first kustom hit the streets, the flame job has been the ultimate poster child of the hot-rod era. While there are a number of ways to do a flame job correctly, there are just as many ways to do a flame job badly. For that reason, there have been entire books written on the subject. A good book to check out, and one of my personal favorites, is Rod Powell's *Flame Painting Techniques.*

Flames are somewhat misleading. The trick to flames is to realize that they must occupy negative and positive space simultaneously in order to balance out the design. In other words, the flames should appear as flames in the positive sense, but in the negative space they should resemble drips. If the drips don't appear balanced, aren't symmetrical, or don't look like drips at all, then your flames are going to suffer as well. The design should also have continuity. Look at the flame in this demo as if it were a body. There's a neck, then a torso, and then two final licks coming out of the top, which could become the neck of a continuing flame. Like juggling, it's a lot easier to demonstrate than to describe.

MATERIALS & EQUIPMENT

3M masking tape
3M 1/8" blue fineline vinyl tape
Red Scotch-Brite pad
X-Acto knife
House of Kolor (Hok) Basecoat Black BC-25
HoK KC20 Post Sanding Cleaner
HoK Hot Pink Pearl Shimrin PBC-39
HoK Violet Kandy Koncentrate KK-17
HoK Intercoat Clear SG-100
HoK striping urethane: Green and Yellow
HoK Reducer RU-311
Xcaliber 000 sword striper
Iwata HP-C top-feed airbrush
Iwata RG-2 touch-up gun
Iwata Eclipse bottle-feed airbrush
Artool freehand shield

1 Using a red Scotch-Brite pad, scuff a powder-coated sign blank. On an actual vehicle, if a paint job is fresh enough, you can use Scotch-Brite for total prepping, but I suggest using 600-grit wet/dry sandpaper because it does a more thorough, even job.

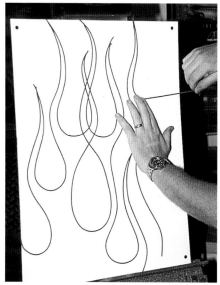

2 Using blue fineline vinyl tape, begin laying out the general pattern of the flames. Working from left to right, focus on the even balance between the body and the licks, or tongues, of the flames. Keep an eye on the negative and positive space to balance the overall design on the board, as well as on the flames themselves.

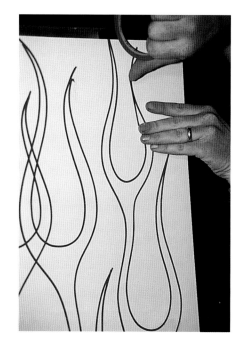

3 When using blue vinyl tape, you must work both hands in unison to pull and place the design. This tape is pressure-sensitive, and while it's repositionable, you can burnish it down to increase the adhesion. Make sure to press especially hard on the ends where they overlap to prevent paint bleeding.

4 With a roll of 3/4" masking tape, begin masking off the flames, butting the tape against the blue fineline. Be sure not to leave any gaps that can allow paint to work its way under the tape.

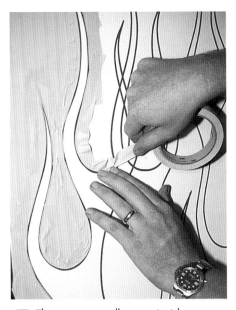

5 The tape can roll on an inside curve, but not an outside curve. By spinning the tape around the design you can mask the flames off quickly without having to cut different sections out. It's important to press the folds down, since they can channel the overspray to the masked off areas like little tunnels.

6 Using an X-Acto knife, cut out the overlapping areas of the blue fineline tape. (The crossover section of the flame will be sprayed with the rest of the design and the overlap will be drop-shadowed later with the airbrush.)

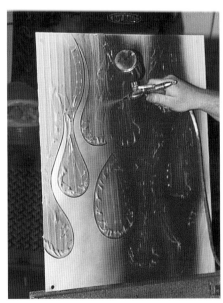

7 Mix a batch of HoK Hot Pink Pearl and use the RG-2 to spray the design. On a full-size vehicle, a larger gun would be better, but for this panel and small helmets or tanks, the RG-2 is just the right size.

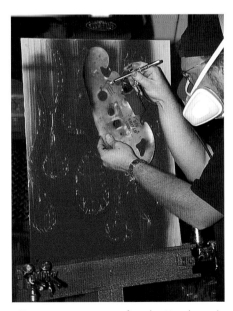

8 Using a mixture of Violet Kandy and intercoat clear, spray the fades onto the tips. Use the freehand shield to help create the weaving effect of the flames while you drop-shadow the corresponding licks. The intercoat clear not only improves the flow of the paint, but also acts as a structural binder to the Violet Kandy toner.

9 Being careful not to peel the paint, remove the masking from the design. Always pull the tape back against itself. This will prevent the tape from lifting and chipping along the tape edge.

10 Using a dry, red Scotch-Brite pad, scuff off any tape residue and eliminate any overspray that may have sneaked through the tape. A little pre-cleaner on a damp towel can also help with this.

11 With the HP-C, mix up a batch of transparent HoK Basecoat Black and lay in the drop shadow of the flame. Create the transparent black by over-reducing the paint. Masking isn't necessary since the transparent black won't discolor the flames too much. (But be careful!)

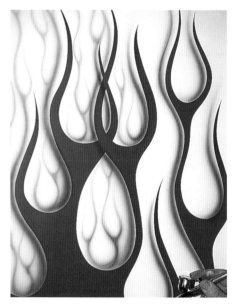

12 To fill in some space, use the transparent Violet Kandy to air-brush in some freehand flames. This not only looks good, but it's a great way to hide any imperfections that you couldn't eliminate with the Scotch-Brite.

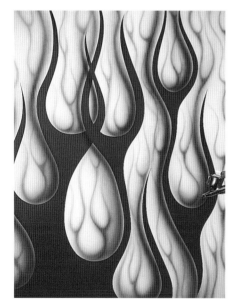

13 Use the violet to go back over the drop shadows too. Remember, always think on your feet when painting. If something doesn't look right, fix it, instead of hoping the client doesn't notice it!

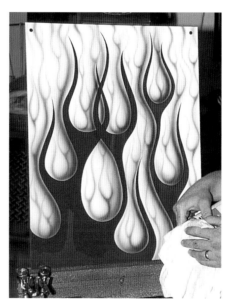

14 Before pinstriping, wipe the entire surface down with a little PPG DX-330 precleaner. You can use any pre-cleaner to remove overspray or tape residue—just be sure it's not too strong, or it will take off all your fades and free-hand flames.

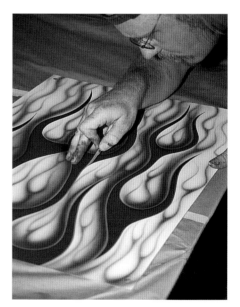

15 Mix a batch of Lime Green strip-ing urethane, by combining HoK Green and a small amount of Lemon Yellow. Carefully pinstripe the outside edge of the flame with a 000 (sword) striper brush. If this were an actual car, you would clearcoat the flames first and then pinstripe the flames between clearcoats. This buries the edge of the flame so that it doesn't peek through the pinstripe. Pinstriping designs on small panels is the best way to build up your pinstriping chops without getting your clients angry.

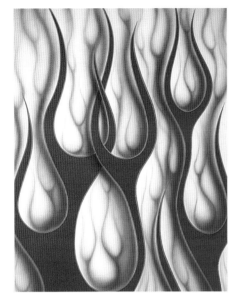

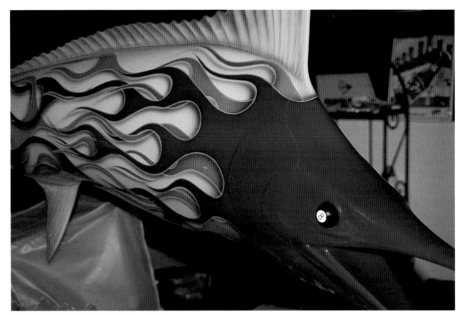

16 And now your flame job is just itchin' to be put on a Street Rod. Practicing is the only way to pick up this technique. And remember, there's no correct style. If your client likes it, the paint doesn't fall off, and small children don't cry when they see it, then you've done your job.

Flame On!

CHAPTER 9

TRIBAL FLAMES

"THE STANDARD FLAME JOB GOES NATIVE"

Tribal graphics have been getting a lot of attention lately, especially the tribal flame design—a hybrid of the classic flame and tribal patterning. This design became popular with the resurgence of the flame job and the popularity of tribal tattooing. Tattoos and tattoo flash art have always been a good source of inspiration for automotive graphics, and vice-versa. I decided to kick this fairly simple design up a notch with a little lizard skin airbrushing. Any graphic can be souped-up with this type of airbrushing. You'll see.

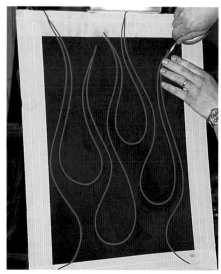

2 Lay out the initial flame design using blue fineline vinyl tape. This step is the same as laying out an ordinary set of flames. It's much easier to lay out the standard classical design of the flames, instead of adding the tribal licks first. Since you're going to add the tribal licks and spikes, make the flames a little more open and spaced farther apart.

3 After the flames are laid out, burnish the tape down to keep it from creeping back and begin adding in the licks and tongues of the tribal patterns. For now, stick to a conservative Polynesian pattern to keep the design less busy. After you get used to the tribal patterning, you can go wild. The vinyl tape is very handy for this, since it's repositionable, allowing you to make a lot of layout mistakes without wasting tape.

1 We painted the sign blank for this demo black to show a flame design over a darker surface, and we masked the border with masking tape. This isn't necessary for the flame design, but looks nice for a presentation piece. It also gives continuity to your demos, in case you're following along and creating a sign blank portfolio.

4 With an X-Acto knife, remove all of the tape overlaps. It's important to realize that the inside of the tapeline is what you're trying to keep clean, not the outside edge. Cut into the original flame to allow the added lick to become a part of the flame body.

5 In the previous flame demo, you learned how to mask out the flames in the traditional way using 3/4" masking tape and paper. For this design, you'll use another technique that's one of my favorites and is good to use on large flat areas where there are little or no curves. Using some Gerber transfer paper, which is used for transferring vinyl lettering, roll and flatten out the transfer tape onto the surface. By rolling and pulling, you can apply the paper with little or no bubbles. The transfer paper is much like contact paper, but less adhesive.

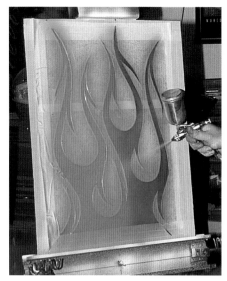

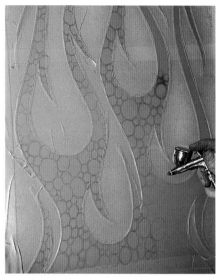

6 With the X-Acto knife, follow the underlying blue tape (you can see it easily through the paper). Carefully cut through the paper, using the blue tape as a buffer to the metal surface. Make sure you don't cut through the paper and tape into the metal surface. This mistake would allow a ghost line to bleed through, possibly damaging the underlying surface, which can cause problems when clearcoating.

7 Using the Iwata RG-2 spray gun with the fan tip, spray an even coat of HoK Shimrin Limetime Pearl Green. The benefit of the Shimrin designer pearls is that the metallic/pearl within the basecoat gives the paint a high level of opacity and covers very well, as you can see over the black. For this same reason, I don't use them for spraying details later on, since the opaque overspray is devastating to the details of a design.

8 With a top-feed airbrush, mix up a batch of HoK Kandy Organic Green Basecoat Koncentrate. This kandy is very transparent, which allows you to build up layers, steadily increasing the detail, depth, and darkness of the design. The snakeskin (as I like to call it) is a conglomeration of differing sizes of circles, intertwined within one another. Although labor intensive to apply, it is definitely a unique space filler for graphics.

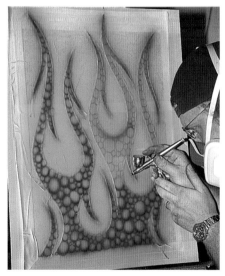

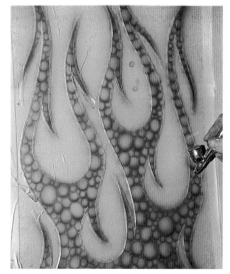

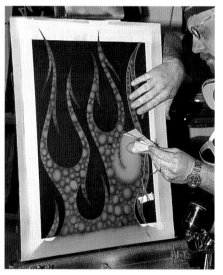

9 After sketching in the faint design, go back over the flames and darken the design, adding shading and shadowing between the circles to emphasize the texture and add depth. Use the same transparent green kandy, just apply it more heavily. The sign of a true kandy is the color's ability to turn almost black when applied in multiple layers.

10 For the final layer, shadow the undersides of the circles to give them individual depth and a slight 3-D appearance. This gives the snakeskin the illusion of having a pebbled surface. To bunch out the larger circles, add a drop of black in the green to speed up the layering process (but not enough black to kill the hue).

11 Give the paint an hour to set and then pull the tape off slowly. Carefully pull back to prevent the paint from lifting. By pulling the tape back against itself, you create a knife-type edge that cuts the paint as you pull, instead of chipping and lifting the paint. Another nice thing about the transfer tape is that you can usually lift the entire masking system with one careful pull (which is a lot better than pulling for a few hours).

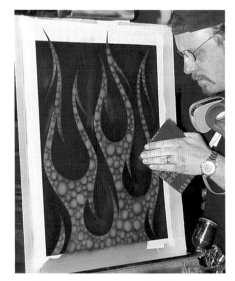

12 Even the most careful of maskers have problems with blowouts and bleed-throughs. The difference between good painters and bad ones is not in how few mistakes they make, but in how they repair the problems. In this case, use a little piece of red Scotch-Brite to scuff off the blow-throughs. Sometimes a rag with a bit of precleaner is all that's necessary to wipe off these annoying overspray demons.

13 Add a small teaspoon of Lazuli dry pearl to some HoK transparent marblizer. Marblizer is a substrate or binding medium that is used as a carrier of dry pearl. It dries slowly, which gives you time to manipulate the surface of the sprayed area.

14 Though you can use anything to manipulate the surface, I decided to use the classic "Ol' School" technique of plastic wrap. While the marblizer is still wet, place the plastic wrap on the surface. The plastic wrap gives an effect similar to that of veins in marble. The effects can vary, depending on the amount of time the plastic is on the surface, or if it is shifted on the surface. If there's a problem with the surface texture, re-spray the area with marblizer, which will reactivate the surface and allow for you to create another effect.

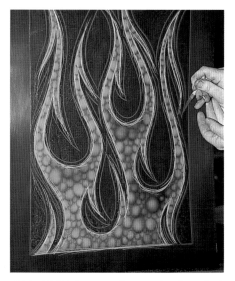

15 Allow the marblizer about half an hour to dry, then spray the entire surface with a protective layer of SG-100 Intercoat Clear. Remove the masking and the piece is ready to be pinstriped. The protective clear is necessary if you have to wipe the pinstriping off without damaging the underlying design. Combine HoK Lite Blue and white striping urethanes and begin striping the flame.

16 Using Lite Blue, begin striping the border edge with a standard Xcaliber 000 sword striper and add a panel effect to the flames. I used a phone book as a palette for the striper to work the paint into the brush. This gives a constant line, and when working on a vehicle, allows you to pull a solid line down an entire length of a car.

17 This is a good example of a tribal flame with a little bit of the Ol' School patterning and some airbrushed goodies. Knowing how to modify a flame design to meet your client's needs will give you a competitive edge and make your designs stand out as your own.

E Pluribus Tribal!

CHAPTER 10

CARBON FIBER TRIBAL

A new graphic style to keep an eye on is "stylized" tribal. Used for over a thousand years in Polynesian religious art, in Celtic art of the medieval period, and in contemporary culture as tattoos, this style has recently increased in popularity among graphic painters. During the past few years, I've noticed a correlation between tattoo work and the new trends in kustoms. With tattooing and kustom painting at an all-time high, it makes sense that the two fields would influence each other.

In this demo, I also decided to incorporate an airbrush effect into the tribal graphic. I achieve this effect by using airbrush and an adhesive stencil system.

2 Begin laying out the tribal pattern with blue vinyl tape. This particular one is along the lines of a stylized Polynesian tattoo. If you were to make it more symmetrical and add a few crossover knotting designs, it would have more of a Celtic look. Some people like to lay down transfer paper and draw the pattern out with pencil. I prefer the free-hand tape method. It makes the design look more natural and less organized and rigid. This is important to retain the organic nature of the tribal pattern (and saves a lot of time in the long run.)

3 When the design layout is complete, use an X-Acto knife to carefully cut away any excess overlaps within the design. If you like, you can add a floating circle in the design, as I did. This is not necessarily a true tribal style, but it does add to the balance of the piece and mimics a little of the Yin-Yang motif.

4 Instead of using 3/4" tape (which would be a nightmare), lay transfer tape over the entire piece and then cut it out with the X-Acto knife. Use a vinyl sign squeegee to smooth out the transfer paper and eliminate any bubbles that can lead to paint bleeds.

2.

3.

1 Mask a standard white sign blank using 3/4" tape to create a border for the design. The border will also give you some leeway in case the edge needs to be trimmed after dings and drops.

4.

MATERIAL & EQUIPMENT

3M masking tape
3M blue fineline vinyl tape
Transferite transparent transfer tape
X-Acto knife
Drywall grid repair tape (adhesive-backed)
House of Kolor (HoK) Black Basecoat BC-25
HoK Tangerine Kandy Koncentrate KK-8
HoK Root Beer Kandy Koncentrate KK-7
HoK Reducer RU-311
HoK Gold, and Orange dry pearl
Hok Real Gold striping urethane
Xcaliber 000 Sword Striper
Iwata HP-C top-feed airbrush
Iwata RG-2 touch-up gun

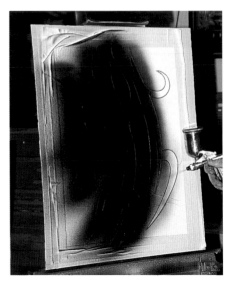

5 Normally, it would not be wise to use an X-Acto to cut out an entire design, but with the blue tape acting as a surface buffer, there's little chance of scoring the underlying paint. But be careful—a cut through the blue tape can cause a nasty paint bleed.

6 To achieve the carbon fiber color, use a black metallic base, almost gunmetal grey. Add a little HoK Graphite pearl to the basecoat black to create the color. When adding the dry pearl it is important to add small quantities at a time and to mix the paint thoroughly. If you add too much at one time, the paint will clog your airbrush and cause spitting.

7 Since you want the pearl to be very heavy, bypass the airbrush and go directly to the RG-2 mini spraygun. Using the fan-tipped RG, spray the entire piece with a standard vertical and horizontal spray pattern. This will give an even surface without any streaks.

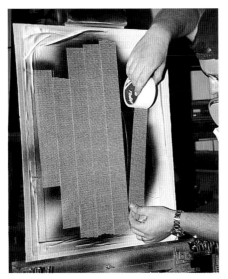

8 Give the paint half-an-hour to dry, then begin laying in the carbon fiber stencil for the second color. The carbon fiber stencil is a good example of borrowing something from a completely separate industry and using it in airbrushing. The sticky back of the drywall repair tape is perfect for positioning on the surface and it easily matches up along the edges for laying out larger areas.

9 When the drywall repair tape is positioned, quickly rub and burnish all of the paintable areas. When using a stencil, contact with the surface is important to prevent paint bleeds and overspray. And with a stencil surface as fine and defined as this one, a little overspray can ruin the entire effect.

10 Mix a combination of black basecoat with a touch of Tangerine Kandy Koncentrate, Root Beer Kandy Koncentrate and a lot of gold pearl. Spray over the stencil to apply the primary color to the carbon fiber. (The black pearl will be the grid of carbon fiber.)

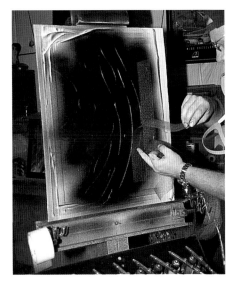

11 Give the paint a few minutes to set, then peel off the dry wall tape stencils to reveal the carbon fiber. Remove any adhesive and overspray from the design with a damp rag of DX-330 Precleaner. This will provide a wet look with which to judge the final effect.

12 Unmask the rest of the design by pulling the tape back against itself to prevent peeling. While adhesion is definitely important, just remember that when the clearcoat is applied, even a graphic with the worst adhesion will be anchored down.

13 With a pure black basecoat (a little over-reduced to make it highly transparent) begin spraying in the drop shadows. This really punches out the piece and gives it an added 3-D "floating" effect.

14 For added definition to your tribal effect, create a background texture. The tribal graphic can contrast and play off this symmetrical pattern, creating additional detail and depth.

15 The final step is the pinstripe. Using your Xcaliber 000 sword striper, carefully pinstripe the tribal edge with HoK "Real Gold" striping urethane.

This classic tribal tattoo pattern with a carbon fiber twist might be an acquired taste, but it's one of the hottest trends in the kustom paint industry today. Whether you combine it with a conservative graphics scheme or use it as the primary style of an entire paint job, the tribal patterns and Celtic knot designs are definitely hittin'. Of course, I can just see myself in 20 years driving around in an electric car with a disgusting pastel basecoat and some really hip Neon graphics wondering what I was thinking. (And no, I won't give an effect for Neon-tube graphics. Some graphic schemes should be allowed to die.)

Go forth and Paint!

CHAPTER 11

FURLING CHECKERS

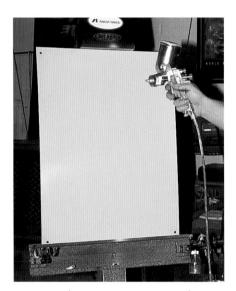

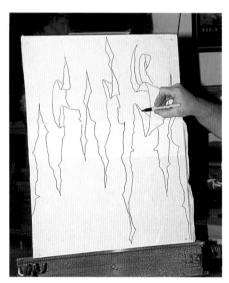

1 Using the Iwata W-88, spray the prepped metal sign blank with HoK SG-101 Lemon Yellow. Since a checkerboard design incorporates both extremes of light and dark (black and white), a bright color like yellow helps to create contrast with the design.

2 After the yellow dries, apply the Gerber transfer tape. By applying it right off the roll, you can eliminate the wrinkling and bubbling that can occur by precutting the paper into sheets. As you've seen in the other demos, you can eliminate these bubbles using a simple vinyl applicator squeegee. If you don't have a vinyl squeegee, you can always use a Bondo spreader.

3 Using a Sharpie pen, lay out the furls and uneven edges of the flag. Even though you'll want the rips and shreds to look completely random, there's still a semblance of order and balance to the design. This is important when laying out graphics on a vehicle. While a little contrast with the design of the vehicle is good, you still need to preserve the lines of the car.

One of the most recognizable designs in automotive graphics, aside from the flame, is the checkerboard pattern. Seen throughout the racing industry, it is the international symbol for winner. Used throughout the kustom paint industry for years, it continues to be a hard-hitting symbol, even in today's newest hybrid styles. But you can even tweak classic symbols a bit to give them a new look

I decided to take this classic international symbol of victory and give it a little twist. I then furled it and shredded it. Okay, I thrashed it. But I created a new style that looks hot on any surface and makes a cool demo. It's a bit labor intensive, so don't commit yourself at first to a large area when painting this design—start with something small like a helmet. But I'll leave that discovery up to you.

4 With a razor blade or X-Acto knife, cut out the design and peel the paper back. Since this entire design must be cut out with a blade (laying out a design like this can be a quick road to insanity), it's important to remember to use a sharp blade. A dull blade will quickly score your paint and may even cause lifting in your graphics.

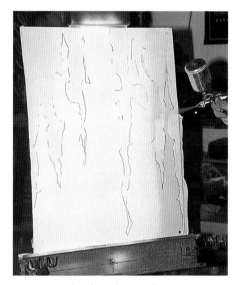

5 Going back to the smaller RG-2 gun, spray down the exposed area with HoK basecoat white. Though you would normally reduce the basecoat in a 1:1 ratio for airbrushing, with the larger spraygun, a ratio of 2:1 (2 parts paint:1 part reducer) provides better coverage.

6 After giving the white coat time to dry, place another sheet of transfer tape over the design on which to lay out the checkers. Due to its high transparency compared to masking tape, the underlying design will be visible and this will help in the layout.

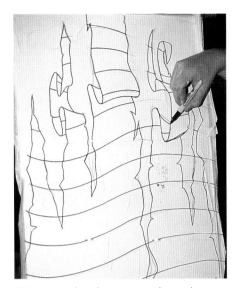

7 Using the Sharpie pen, begin laying out the checkerboard design. To make the furl effect more realistic, give the checkerboard pattern a slight curve. The rule of thumb here is that no matter what direction and shape you give the pattern, you must keep the checked boxes consistent in size.

8 Give the vertical grid a slight curve to mimic the horizontal lines. Notice how even though the shapes of the checks vary, the sizes remain similar. A slight variation can give a 3-D effect, but too much will just make the layout look sloppy. Mark the checked boxes to be removed with an "X." This may sound simplistic, but trust me, it's easy to make a cutting mistake at this stage.

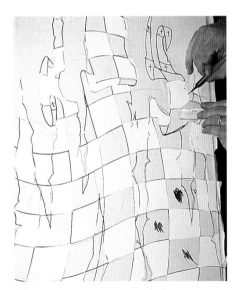

9 Cut one more time with the X-Acto knife. (This is definitely a demo where, if you weren't good with a blade before this graphic, you'll be an expert by the time you're done.) If this were a straight checkerboard, you would layer 1" tape to form the grid, a faster method that lessens the amount of cutting.

10 Cleaning the white out of the mini-gun, spray the masked checks with basecoat black. The RG-2 is the perfect gun for small graphics such as this, since it's easy to clean, doesn't spray too much material, and the tape edge doesn't get too coated.

11 At this point it can get confusing. When there is a double masking system involved, it's important to make sure you don't pull the wrong piece of tape. Of course, you can always re-mask any mistake with a bit of scrap tape. (Don't beat yourself up over it.)

12 Mix a combination of Violet and Cobalt Blue Kandy and spray in some streaks and shadows to give the flag an added furled effect. A touch of Lazuli Blue dry pearl added to the mix gives the flag a nice glow too. Little touches like this keep your graphics looking fresh and different.

13 To create tight furls and darker shadows, add a little black to the violet mix in the HP-C, and pick up the freehand shield to help keep the lines sharp, but soft. (Be careful with the black at this stage; too much will muddy up the checker design, and you'll lose the sharp effect you created with your masking.)

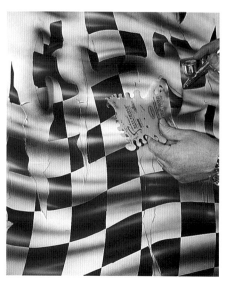

14 When airbrushing, white is even more dangerous than black where overspray is concerned. While white improves the flag's three dimensionality 100%, it can also wipe out the design if you use it too much. Remember the rule of all design (I can't say it enough): Less is more.

15 Once the airbrushing is done in the flag design, unmask the shreds and wipe down the entire surface with precleaner. It's important to get all the residue removed. Any glue, overspray, or dirt will not only show up when cleared, but will probably be amplified.

16 As a transition color between the checkered flag and the yellow background, airbrush in a mixture of Tangerine Kandy and intercoat clear. A little Lavender Pearl in the mix adds to the background glow and ties in with the violet of the checkers.

17 Add a touch of basecoat black to the tangerine and bring in the drop shadows of the design to give the shreds one more added illusion of furling and floating above the yellow background. Of all the techniques that are important to master in automotive airbrushing, drop shadows are in the top three. Not because it's the most important effect, but because it's difficult to keep a gradated fade clean. An airbrusher's ability is often judged on this simple technique. No freehand stencil can help you with this.

CHAPTER 12

18 Like many of the effects in this book, the final step before clearing is pinstriping. Using HoK Silver urethane striping enamel, lay on the stripe with a #1 Mack lettering quill. On tight corners and curves, the fastest and cleanest brushes are often the short-haired quills and not the sword stripers.

While this graphic my be a far cry from the conservative classic checkerboard, these little twists are often what make the client happy. No one wants his kustom looking like everyone else's. Each technique demonstrated in this book can be broken down and combined to form any design at any level of style, from absolute "Ol' School" conservative to kolor wheel nightmares—this is up to you.

Carpe paintum!

MATERIAL & EQUIPMENT

Transferite transfer tape
Sharpie pen
X-Acto knife
House of Kolor (HoK) Basecoat Black
   BC-25
HoK Lemon Yellow Basecoat SG-101
HoK Basecoat White BC-26
HoK Violette Kandy Koncentrate KK-17
HoK Cobalt Blue Kandy Koncentrate
   KK-5
HoK Tangerine Kandy Koncentrate KK-8
HoK Reducer RU-311
HoK Metallic Silver striping urethane
#1 Mack lettering quill
Iwata HP-C top-feed airbrush
Iwata RG-2 touch-up gun
Artool Freehand shield

SPACE, THE FINAL FRONTIER

(WELL, NOT QUITE FINAL...JUST CHAPTER 12)

It's important to learn how to create filler—the stuff airbrushed within graphics for added effect, or in the background of a mural to fill space. Most of the effects in this book are filler, but the granddaddy of all filler is outer space. Space, stars, and planets have been used for years by such greats as Frank Frazetta and Boris Vallejo.

Outer space filler shouldn't be used solely to take up space (no pun intended), but should aid in the composition and theme of the piece. For reference, you can use anything from encyclopedias and star charts to *Star Trek* movies (my favorite). The opening sequence in *Next Generation* and *Voyager* have some of the best space images I've seen. (Although nothing quite resembles the Mutara nebula in *Wrath of Khan*.)....I'm such a geek!

1 For the starfield, mask the border of your sign blank, then spray the entire surface with an even coat of HoK Basecoat Black urethane. Allow half-an-hour to dry, then scuff the surface with a wet, red Scotch-Brite pad. This will knock down the shine and give the surface a good tooth for the colors and final clearcoat.

2 To create the planets and moons, use a simple circular template. (Make sure it's urethane-proof or it might buckle. Berel's architecture templates are sturdy.) If you'd rather not use a commercial template, you can always use a roll of tape for an instant circle template. (Now you know why most of the circles in my murals are the same size.) Determine the placement of the planet and moon, then spray them in using HoK Basecoat White.

3 After removing the template, notice how I sprayed the white more heavily on one side. This establishes the light source in the lower left-hand corner. You could use the popsicle stick method to stipple in stars, but you must maintain more control here, (stars on top of planets don't look too cool) so, pull back the trigger, without air, and load the needle with paint. After releasing the trigger and hitting air, you'll acheive a nice supernova. (This trick only works with gravity-feed airbrushes; siphon-feeds require lower pressure.)

4 Of course, anyone who's seen *Star Trek* knows that space isn't made up of stars alone. For extra effect, you've got to add all those gas clouds and spiral galaxies. Using the basecoat white, fog in the clouds and add halo effects around a few of the primary stars.

5 Keeping the light source in mind, create several impact craters and features on the moon's surface. Remember to keep a good overall balance in your design while working. It's easy to clutter up one corner of a design when you're trying to paint randomly.

6 To give a cool effect to the gas cloud at the bottom of this design, I added a little HoK Blue/Pink marblizer with some silver dry pearl. Instead of spraying it on the surface first, I sprayed it onto plastic wrap, and then pressed it against the design while still wet. This gave a tighter, marbled effect and added a lot of depth to the gas nebula when cleared. Give it a try.

7 By wadding the plastic wrap into different shapes, you can continue manipulating the marblizer in the nebula until you get the right look.

8 Now you're ready to add color. First, mix transparent HoK Magenta Kandy with intercoat clear and HoK Lavender Pearl. Since it's transparent, the magenta will only show up over the white areas. The first layer of white is just an undercoat for the subsequent colors. A major benefit of working with transparents over black is reduced overspray. (Keep the air pressure between 20 to 30 psi!!)

9 Mix a batch of transparent HoK Cobalt Blue. Color in the surrounding gas clouds and add a little depth to the distant stars by fogging blue over them. This will make them look farther away. Use the blue also to give the moon a primarily blue glow and to build up the main details of the craters and shadows. Since the blue is also transparent, it combines nicely with the magenta to give a light purple effect to the surrounding clouds. (One of the few times that transparency can work to your advantage.)

10 After bringing in a little violet to darken the moon and add some more color, bring back the stars with white. Since all of the stars were previously muted with color, the contrast to the flecked white is immediate. It punches out the design, giving it an incredible sense of depth. For even more depth, black toner can be sprayed into areas to give the gas clouds some inclusions or even a black hole or two. Be careful not to deaden your design with the black though. Again, less is more!

11 And there you have it: a pretty hip space scene. Just clear it and it's finished. Besides making a cool backdrop to graphics and murals, starfields are great space fillers for lettering or even painted effects for vinyl.

Paint long and prosper!

CHAPTER 13

STYLIZED CHROME
THE AIR SYNDICATE WAY

The chrome effect is popular in air-brushing, and often overused in lettering and commercial illustration. The original chrome effect has its roots in the 1960s with the early work of Ed Newton, and later in the illustrations, cartoons, and fine artwork of Robert Williams. In this demo, I'm not going to render a photorealistic chrome; instead, I'm going to develop a more stylized one. My version exaggerates the technique of the chrome, giving it a ruddy, cartoonish appearance. This style of chrome reads well from a distance—a good trait for both cars and signage, since both must read well up close and from afar. It has a very flashy appearance and, because of its busy texture, is almost impossible to screw up.

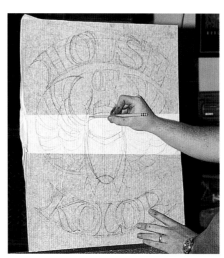

2 Give the basecoat about half-an-hour to dry, then apply a sheet of transfer tape and lay out the design in pencil. The best part about using transfer tape is that, if you make mistakes, you can just erase them before cutting out the design.

3 When you're satisfied with the design, finalize the layout with a felt-tip pen. This will give you a line to follow with the X-Acto knife.

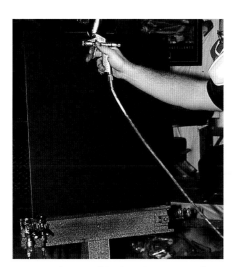

1 Prep the sign blank with a piece of 600-grit wet/dry sandpaper, then spray the background with HoK Shimrin Passion Pearl basecoat. Instead of loading the large spray gun, continue to use the Iwata RG-2 for these medium jobs. It's also an excellent choice for small graphics and fades as well.

4 When using an X-Acto knife, or any razor edge for that matter, it's important to make sure it is sharp, especially when working on a metallic surface. The reason for this is that a dull blade will more readily score the surface, which can cause problems when clearcoating. Because of this, rarely, if ever, use a blade on the actual car surface if you can help it.

5 Using the Iwata Eclipse, spray the exposed areas with HoK BC-26 Basecoat White. If the graphic is too large and needs an even finish (such as a transparent kandy), then a fan-headed spray gun would be a better choice.

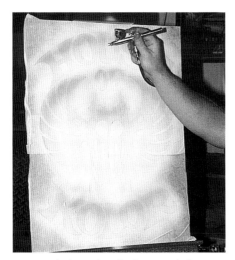

6 With the airbrush, fog in a light layer of Kandy Oriental Blue. When airbrushing chrome, you must realize that the actual color of the chrome will reflect whatever is in the surrounding area. In a stylized, cartoony chrome, such as this one, go with a classic horizon line and sky reflection, basically blue, with a few earth tones, as in the horizon line.

7 Mix a batch of red oxide (a half-and-half mixture of root beer and tangerine kandy concentrate, with inter-coat clear as a binder.) The red oxide makes a good horizon line and, because it's transparent, you can build up different values of the same color just by layering it (you can't do this with an opaque).

8 Create a number of thin lines and varying reflections to give the chrome effect a compound-curved look. (A flat machined chrome surface would show uniform, horizontal reflections and horizon lines.) With all the multiple curves, the surface now resembles liquid mercury. This technique is key when rendering chrome on a curved bumper or grill.

9 To add a little color and to darken the top edge of the chrome's horizon line, mix a batch of transparent Kandy Violet. Transparent violet has the tendency to appear as true violet when applied over white; yet, when applied over the red oxide color, it appears to be deep brown, almost black.

10 Since the majority of the original white has been compromised by overspray, apply some white from the Eclipse bottle, using the Iwata HP-C top-feed. (Switch to the HP-C for added detail and lower overspray.) Apply the white only on the high sides of the chrome, at the top edge of the horizon line. Notice how the chrome is taking on more of a 3-D appearance now with the white highlights.

11 When the primary airbrushing is done, carefully peel off the transfer tape. As a rule of thumb, try not to leave any masking system on a vehicle for more than a few days, and never leave a masked car in the sun. The heat from the sun, as well as extended mask time, can leave marks on the original basecoat, or worse yet, lift the paint or blush the surface. Always wipe the surface with precleaner after removing the masking system. This eliminates any trace elements of adhesive from your painting or clearcoating.

12 Using a mixture of HoK Basecoat Black BC-25 and Violet Kandy concentrate, airbrush in the drop shadows of the chrome logo. This drop shadow effect not only adds to the apparent depth of the piece, but also hides any rough design edges and covers any airbrushed bleeds that may have occurred along the cut edge. Remember when airbrushing a drop shadow, no true shadow is black; it is merely the underlying color with a reduced amount of light. Shadows are not truly "cast," but they are light that is "blocked." By using the transparent mixture of black and violet, you will allow the underlying Passion Pearl basecoat to come through.

13 Coming back to the white, notice how I pop out some highlights along the edges and tips of the HoK "Scarab" beetle wings. The overspray from the highlights looks like the actual halo that a reflection might give off. This is a good example of how one can use the drawbacks to an airbrush (overspray for one) to act as an advantage in rendering. Simply put, let a problem work for you. Remember, half of the innovative effects in this book were designed more by accident than design.

14 Using HoK silver striping urethane, outline the design with a #1 lettering quill. Before lettering, clear the panel once, then sand the surface to eliminate the edge. This provides a cleaner surface to stripe. We make it a practice at Kal Koncepts to clearcoat before every striping job. If not, the sharp edge of the masked graphic can peek through, creating a messy stripe after clearcoating.

MATERIALS & EQUIPMENT

Transferite transfer tape
HB pencil
Marker pen
X-Acto Knife
House of Kolor (HoK) Basecoat White BC-26
HoK Basecoat Black BC-25
HoK Oriental Blue Kandy Koncentrate KK-4
HoK Violet Kandy Koncentrate KK-17
HoK Tangerine Kandy Koncentrate KK-8
HoK Root Beer Kandy Koncentrate KK-7
HoK Intercoat Clear SG-100
Hok Reducer RU-311
HoK Metallic Silver striping urethane
#1 lettering quill
Iwata Hp-C top-feed airbrush
Iwata Eclipse CS top-feed airbrush
Iwata Eclipse bottle-feed airbrush
Iwata RG-2 touch-up gun

15 After the striping is finished, allow an hour or two to set. (HoK does dry within a half hour, but I recommend giving the paint a little longer to cure.) This is the best way to ensure a good clearcoat, and prevent bleeding and pulling. Next, apply a tack coat, followed by three wet coats of HoK UFC-40 urethane clear. Allowing 24 hours to set, the clear can then be color sanded and buffed to perfection.

While there are many different ways to stylize chrome, this is a fun and quick way to create graphics or logo designs and to give the ordinary chrome effect a bit of a tweak.

Keep on Chromin'!

CHAPTER 14

CHROME CHOPPER LOGO

We've learned how to use transfer tape, vinyl squeegees, and even computer-cut masking vinyl. But, we haven't yet learned to use vinyl as a visual in a graphic. I don't recommend using vinyl as an actual graphic element when clearcoating, but sometimes there are a few effects that can't be accomplished without it. One of these effects is a true chrome effect or mirror finish. We won't actually use vinyl, but rather a chrome Mylar with a protective coating. The same concept works for both, however. A 1.5 mil exterior chrome Mylar will be used for the main element of this logo design.

Jesse James of West Coast Choppers of California asked me to design and paint a logo on his show trailer. The paint job called for a tribal flame design across the length of the sides, with Jesse's "Coop Devil" character pointing toward the logo. The logo itself consisted of a 5-foot-wide chrome Maltese cross with the West Coast Choppers name included. I decided to first experiment on a smaller scale to master the mirror effect and to see how it would clearcoat.

MATERIALS & EQUIPMENT

3M masking tape
Transfer tape
Chrome Mylar or high performance vinyl
Vinyl squeegee
X-Acto knife
House of Kolor (HoK) Basecoat White
   BC-26
HoK Tru-Blu Shimrin Basecoat PBC-36
HoK Violette Kandy Koncentrate KK-17
HoK Oriental Blue Kandy UK-04
HoK Intercoat Clear SG-100
HoK Lite Blue and White striping
   urethanes
HoK Reducer RU-311
Artool Skullmaster freehand shield
Piece of photo paper for ripped cloud
   mask
#1 Mack lettering quill
Iwata HP-C top-feed airbrush
Iwata RG-2 touch-up gun.

1 What a surprise, one more masked sign blank! Using the RG-2 again, spray on an even coat of HoK Tru-Blu Shimrin. Beginning with a light-tack coat, build up even layers to eventually cover the entire board with color.

2 By first spraying in horizontal patterns, then vertical columns, you can cover the entire board with little patterning. Using this crisscross technique of layering, a small gun with limited coverage can evenly cover a large area.

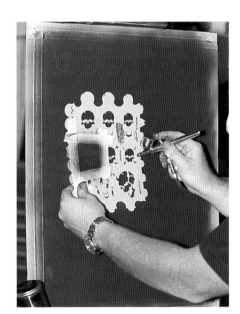

3 When satisfied with the color, lay in a pattern of skulls for the background landscape with the Artool Skullmaster shield. Spray the skulls with a mixture of the same Tru-Blu Shimrin, with Violette Pearl added to give the skulls a glimmer at certain viewing angles. These are appropriately known as ghost images or ghosting.

4 Using precleaner (wiping between each step will keep your piece clean), wipe the surface to eliminate the overspray, but also to obtain a wet look, so you can see how the pearled skulls are going to look when cleared.

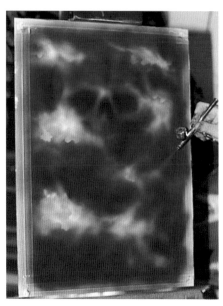

5 Mix some pure white basecoat for the HP-C and lay in some clouds to create a patterned background for the chopper logo. (While this is not the same background being used for the trailer, I decided to throw in a small cloud demo just for the fun of it.)

6 With the loose cloud pattern airbrushed, use a cloud stencil to create a few clean, soft edges to define the shapes. You can make one from torn cardboard. The torn edges give a more natural feathered edge than you can get from cutting with a blade. Old 8" x 10" photographs work too and they resist urethane paints fairly well.

7 Darken the clouds and add extra depth to the sky scene with Oriental Blue kandy. (Yes, that is a skull outlined in the clouds. Clouds are a good source of hidden designs because of their random shapes.)

8 To create a central light source, use the circle template to airbrush a moon silhouette behind the clouds. Normally, you should mask off the surrounding area of the template, but with all the clouds in the background, any overspray will be lost.

9 Using the same basecoat white, spray in patterned moonbeams breaking through the clouds. Add small amounts of white to the surrounding clouds to emphasize the reflection of the beams. This adds depth and increases the realism of the cloud scene.

10 Add a bit of violet to the Oriental Blue to darken the backs of the clouds. This not only darkens up and hides any overspray, but emphasizes the whiteness of the light source by creating contrast. You can see how playing back and forth with a few transparent colors can truly build the depth.

11 Cut a square of chrome Mylar and apply a sheet of transfer tape to one side. Sketch out the logo and ink it in preparation for cutting. Tape the top edge of the Mylar square to hold it in the center position (directly over the airbrushed moon). Remove the adhesive backing and smooth slowly into place.

12 When applying 5-foot sheets of this material, apply it wet without the transfer tape, using a cotton covered squeegee to remove the water. This helps remove the bubbles and creases without scratching the Mylar surface. Because you have to wait for the trapped water to absorb and dry in the glue before clearcoating, the wet technique takes a bit longer.

13 Using the X-Acto knife, cut and peel out the letters of the logo, much as would be done on a full-scale job. Granted, you'll probably go through about a hundred times more blades. (This Mylar does love to eat the blades.)

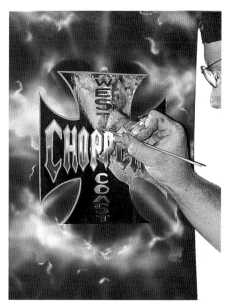

14 After you peel the letters off, remove the protective sheet of transfer tape. Now you can see why the moon was put in the middle of the logo. The bright white center allows the letters to be read more easily, plus it helps in centering the letters.

15 Mix a combination of HoK Lite Blue striping urethane with a little white to obtain process blue. Outline the letters, working with the #1 letter quill.

After clearcoating, any small scratches on the mirrored surface disappear and the chrome takes on a nice shine. While this demo proved successful, it also pointed out a flaw that I didn't think about. The Mylar is so thin, it shows anything underneath it—dust, paint nibs, tape edges, you name it. So for the main piece, the underlying paint will be sanded first. The added help of the water for positioning and smoothing ought to take care of this goose-bump effect (plus, I imagine a few gallons of clear will help even out the playing field as well).

Since the vinyl/Mylar we're using only has a 5-year warranty, that's also going to be the extent of our paint warranty. But I have a feeling that with the added UV protection, we may be able to buy a few more years before it starts to go bad (if it even does.) This is the type of gambling you do as a kustom painter and, on average, it works out for you. If it doesn't, bite your tongue, fix the job, and chalk it up to education.

Paint ya' later!

CHAPTER 15

DIAMOND PLATIN'

Kustom painters not only have to deliver quality at a competitive price, but they also have to keep up with the newest styles and hip F/X. To stay in the business, painters must have a pulse on the latest trend, or take the initiative to lead the pack by experimenting and creating their own F/X. However, constant experimentation can take a toll on a painter's work. One shortcut to innovation is to take what is common practice in another industry and adopt it.

A good example of this is seen in the vinyl graphics field. The technology that sign makers have used for years has now found its way into the automotive industry in the form of predesigned vinyl graphics. But the great thing about this industry is that, no matter how innovative an idea may appear, there are always ways to improve upon it. For example, vinyl will never replace graphics, no matter how much a painter airbrushes on it. Most people will always view them as stickers. The trick is to use vinyl technology to improve

the one aspect of the industry that has shown little development in the last 20 years—masking. Bob Bond pioneered this concept with his Splash mask system, and he and many others contributed to CD ROM graphics packages such as Vector Art's systems.

In the previous chapters, we learned about the techniques for airbrushing granite, wood, marble, etc. Now I'll show you how to combine computer design programs, vinyl cutters, and airbrushing into the Diamond Plate effect—once extremely time-consuming and a major pain in the butt.

Of all the automotive effects I've rendered, this is one of the few that was borrowed from the illustration field. About six years ago, I was staring at our boat trailer at Kal Koncepts and I thought, "That would look trippy in a graphic or as a background effect." I debuted it in the 1996 Ford Prototype F-150 that we painted and displayed at the SEMA show several years ago. I created that effect using a freehand

2 Another company that found it amusing to give an airbrusher expensive things to play with was Roland. (Thanks to David who loaned me a Roland Camm 1 to experiment with my vinyl cutting.) Using my trusty Gerber mask, the Camm 1 cut the 18" x 24" mask (a few hundred diamond patterns or so) in about the time it would take me to hand cut a 20-diamond stencil.

shield and many hours (the orange Mazda in our paint video took five hours of using a freehand stencil). But this newly modified demo will explain how the computer can be used to take all the drudgery out of positioning, layout, and cutting your design without using a soggy, dog-eared stencil and masking tape.

MATERIALS & EQUIPMENT

3M masking tape
Flexi-sign vinyl design and cutting
 program
Roland Camm 1 cutter/plotter
Sony VAIO 200 MHz 3-gig PC (your
 computer may vary)
X-Aacto knife
Plastic vinyl squeegee
Transfer tape
Circle template
House of Kolor (HoK) Orion Silver
 Basecoat BC-02
HoK Basecoat Black BC-25
HoK Tangerine Kandy Koncentrate KK8
HoK Root Beer Kandy Koncentrate
 KK-7
HoK Intercoat Clear SG-100
HoK Baseocoat White BC-26
HoK Reducer RU-311
Artool Freehand Shield
Iwata HP-C top-feed airbrush
Iwata RG-2 touch-up Gun

1 Using Amiable Technologies Flexi-Sign Pro sign design program, I was able to work up a Diamond Plate design that closely resembled the plate of our boat trailer. The design included a small border around each piece that the plotter would cut out. This border mask is used to show the beveled edge created when Diamond Plate is punched out during fabrication (another big thanks to Joe Calabrese of Air Graphix, Inc., Toms River, New Jersey—without his help with my computer gauntlet, I'd be toast.)

3 Once again, prepare the surface of your sign blank for painting. (I get these metal blanks from a buddy who works at a sign shop. There are usually over-runs, and you can pick them up cheaply for test panels or demo boards. This particular sign blank already had a white powder coating on it, so it didn't need any primer.) Take a red Scotch-Brite pad and scuff the sheen to give the paint some tooth to stick to. Wipe the surface with precleaner to remove any oils or contaminants.

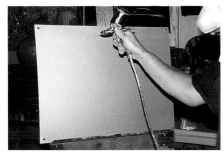

4 Using the Iwata RG-2 touchup gun, spray an even coat of HoK's Orion Silver basecoat. This gives the diamond plate a good metallic base to heighten the realism of the finish. (Notice the respirator I'm wearing. Anytime I airbrush or paint urethanes in my shop, I wear a good dual-cartridge respirator rated for organic vapors, in addition to a good ventilation system. Because of some of the caustic pigments in many of the "non-toxic" water-based paints, it's a good idea to wear a mask when you're using them, too. Better safe than sorry.)

5 Switching to the Iwata HP-C top-feed airbrush, create water-stain marks, streaking, and distress marks in the metal surface using over-reduced HoK Black Basecoat mixed with a little silver. Whenever working over a metallic surface like silver, it's a good idea to add a little of the original silver into any of your opaque pigments. This gives the paint a similar incidence of refraction with the light source. In short, without the silver, any opaque paint will appear to float above the metal surface.

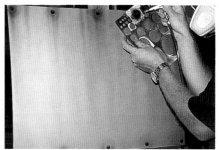

6 Using a masked-off architectural circle template, lay in some rivets along the top and bottom. This not only helps the metal panel effect, but also hides any drill holes that were already in the panel. (Didn't know they were there until I opened the box. Like I always say, you can make something out of anything. Airbrushers don't make mistakes...we just change our minds a lot!) Using the same black/silver mixture, make sure it is overly reduced to prevent any of the airbrushing from standing out too much. After all, it is the background treatment.

7 To bring a little color into the piece, create some rust deterioration. This is accomplished using a mixture of HoK Tangerine and Root Beer Kandy Koncentrates. Since these koncentrates are transparent kandies, there's no need to add the silver for it to blend in with the piece. The silver underneath will come through due to the transparency factor. This color can also be achieved using PPG Red Oxide. Though I only mention certain brands when I'm spraying, this is because it's what we use at our shop. Just about all kolors used in any of my demos can be closely matched by many of the other toner systems on the market. (Just tryin' to be unbiased.)

8 With the underlying metal treatment done, cut off a section of the pre-cut diamond plate mask. Borrowing an old signmaker's trick (from my buddy Joe in Toms River again), lay the sheet on the board using the "butterfly" technique. This is where you first center the design, then tape the middle, and peel each side independently before sticking it to the surface. Not only is this technique a major time saver in aligning a piece, but it helps to prevent a lot of nasty bubbles that have a tendency to show up at inopportune moments.

9 Using a plastic vinyl squeegee, burnish the vinyl into the surface before unmasking the transfer tape and get rid of any rogue bubbles, or at least flatten them to prevent any paint bleeding.

10 With the surface smooth and all the bubbles sent to bubble hell, carefully remove the transfer tape. The "carefully" is important in this step; if you get too gung-ho, you can accidentally remove half of your vinyl masking as well. For the "sign illiterate" (like me), the transfer tape is used to hold the cut vinyl together while pulling off the backing paper and allows you to transfer the design to the surface, then peel it away so you can get to the masked area. (Pretty kewl. What will these sign guys think of next?)

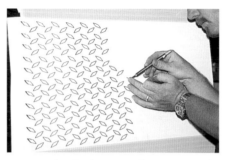

11 Now the fun part of signage work, the weeding. (The real reason they call it weeding is because it's about as much fun as weeding the lawn.) Using an X-Acto knife, lift out all of the individual borders that the computer cut around the initial diamond design. These are going to be painted a lighter color, with the surrounding area remaining masked, to give the illusion of an external light source reflecting off of them.

12 Notice the top and bottom of the board is masked off to prevent any overspray. This is important, especially when using silver. (That stuff loves to float around and stick on important surfaces, and not show up until after it's cleared.) Using the same HP-C, spray a mixture of silver and white on the unmasked beveled area.

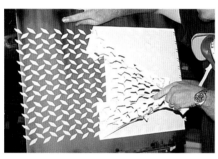

13 After giving the paint about 15 minutes to set, begin pulling away the mask. The mask used in this project is Gerber Mask. The Gerber Mask is one of the most resistant to urethanes and peels away easily without lifting the underlying colors. I do recommend removing the masking as soon as it's painted on to prevent the urethane from hardening the vinyl, which can cause a problem with removal.

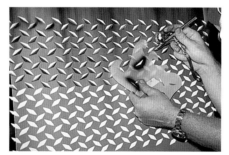

14 Here's a good example of what can happen when you're too busy running back and forth with your camera and airbrush and you forget a step. I was so excited about getting the masking off (the funnest part of painting), that I forgot to hit the bottom edge of the bevel with my black/silver mixture for the underlying, shadowed side of the diamond. Don't worry, it's not ruined, and I'm definitely not going to re-mask everything! Cutting a small triangle shape out of my Artool shield that matches the bottom edge of the diamond, I fall back on the tried and true method of freehand masking and individually spraying each diamond.

15 To give the diamonds an added sense of depth, freehand in a gradated drop shadow under each one. For the drop shadow, use a transparent black solution with no silver since you want the shadow to have no opacity, just merely darken the existing area. The center diamond faces are still masked, so you don't have to worry about overspray on the top areas from the shadowing. No matter what masking system you use, you should always add freehand touches. This not only softens the edges, but will add a personalized touch to your work and prevent your finished piece from looking like an airbrushed sticker.

  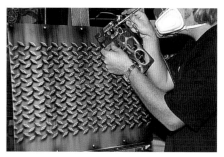

16 With the freehand airbrush sculpting done, remove the remainder of the masking from the diamond centers. After all of the unmasking is completed, wipe the entire surface with a cloth dampened with water and precleaner. This will remove any adhesive residues and overspray that may have stuck to the surface. Don't make it a point to scrub the surface. You don't want to rub off your airbrushed shading.

17 Going back with a transparent mixture of Black and Rootbeer toner, continue some of the streaks down the surface. Again, this freehanding will blend in the hard masked areas and since the urethane toners are transparent, the detailed edges will show through, adding to the realism and three-dimensionality of the design. Plus, it fools all of the masking gurus and frisket freaks into thinking you did multiple layers of masking to get all the varied colors and shades. Remember, keep it easy. In the immortal words of Mies Vanderow: "Less is More." Really, how complicated can diamond plate be?

18 Using the circle template one final time, I hit a small highlight on the top round of every rivet with the airbrush and silver/white mixture used earlier, just a little more over-reduced. Be careful when making these final touches. The last thing you want to do is kill your piece with too many highlights or white highlight overspray. I left the individual diamonds alone.

19 Well, there you have it: a nice example of how to render a realistic effect using combined media. Apply a coat of clear and you've got a great demo panel to hang on your wall or take to shows. Playing with sign blanks will give you a good stockpile of examples for your clients to check out when deciding on a graphic job, and will also provide a good practice surface, without having to experiment on the 350-lb. Harley owner's pride and joy. (Did I mention the health benefits of this?)

This vinyl system of masking opens new doors of painting previously ignored because of the tedium or impossibility of masking. However, it can also be a trap. Freehand techniques are just as important, if not more so, when working with masking to protect against the sticker look. Freehand shields and moveable masks are still important tools for touch-ups.

I can't guarantee that vinyl masking systems, CD ROM graphic files, and computer generated designs are the answer to every painter's masking dilemma. But they are useful tools that elevate the quality of a kustom paint job to another level. It's important to note that using vinyl doesn't make you an automotive painter, just as using Photoshop doesn't make you an artist—it's an important addition to your arsenal of time-saving tricks.

Innovate, don't imitate.

CHAPTER 16

STRETCHED FACES

What F/X manual would be complete without a demo on painting tortured faces pressing through toxic green plastic wrap? If you don't find these images frightening, picture them poking through your wallpaper or bathroom mirror at 3 a.m.!

I've painted this effect several times during the past six years, but just recently I've had a number of requests for it. This demo is a bit tricky because you're creating a positive element by airbrushing in the negative space. (I know, that darn negative/positive stuff again...sorry.) In the finished piece, the lightest areas of the image that appear closer to you are actually the underlying green color. To create the illusion of depth, you can make these colors appear lighter and bring them forward by airbrushing in the surrounding shadows of the stretched fabric. It follows along the depth theory that light colors come forward and dark colors recede. If you've got an existing light colored area, and you bring it forward by darkening the surrounding areas, then you are airbrushing in the negative space to create design depth.

Use the demo as an example, but also try to render different objects with this stretched effect, including lettering.

MATERIALS & EQUIPMENT

3M masking tape
White greaseless/waxless chalk
Skull model or photograph
House of Kolor (HoK) Basecoat
   Limetime Shimrin PBC-38
Hok Basecoat White BC-26
HoK Basecoat Black BC-25
HoK Kandy Organic Green
   Koncentrate KK-9
HoK Intercoat Clear SG-100
HoK Reducer RU-311
Iwata HP-C top-feed airbrush
Iwata RG-2 touch-up gun
Iwata HP-C top-feed .2mm airbrush
Artool freehand shield

1 First, sand your sign blank and mask the border. To create the toxic green background, spray with a good coat of HoK Limetime Shimrin urethane. These Shimrins have a cool pearlescent effect that changes color depending on the light source. You can also use other colors; just remember that if they're too dark, the detail work is hard to see.

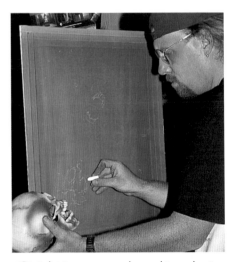

2 I don't recommend stretching plastic wrap over a friend's face as a reference source, but you can obtain a similar effect with wet cheesecloth, and your model won't die from asphyxiation. For this demo, I used a photo of a face behind a sheet and a model skull. Lightly sketch the design on the sign blank with white chalk.

3 Using HoK BC-26 Basecoat White and the Eclipse, freehand spray all the highlights of the faces, fingertips, and folds. It's important not to go overboard with the white at this stage; if you do, it could clutter the piece. Also, make sure the white is thinned enough so that it still covers but doesn't leave any grainy spray. Very little chalk was used in the sketch due to the transparent nature of this design.

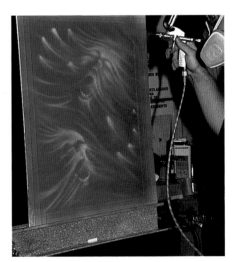

4 With Limetime Shimrin and the RG-2, fog over the white highlights with metallic green. This not only blends the design into the background, but also mutes the white so that it doesn't stand out as much. Keeping the light source to the right, fog the left side of the images more to give the illusion of cast shadows.

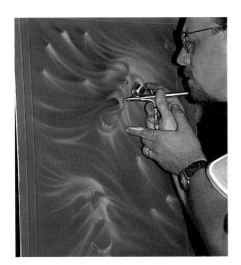

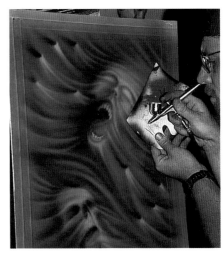

5 Allow the Shimrin half-an-hour to dry. Using the HP-C, begin defining the shadows and folds with Kandy Organic Green Koncentrate mixed with SG-100 intercoat clear. This highly transparent solution has enough pigment to color, but still allows the metallic to show through. The trick to airbrushing shadows is that you must visualize the design in the negative in order to airbrush around the highlights.

6 Moving to the HP-C .2mm detail gun, darken the solution with a bit of black toner. This speeds up the layering process and adds more depth, especially around the teeth and fingertips, where more contrast is needed to punch them out. A movable photo-paper mask is used to give a cleaner, hard line to the dark sides of the folds and wrinkles. Keeping the shield slightly off the surface prevents the line from appearing too hard and masked.

7 With the transparent green, soften the shielded lines and finish any final details and touch-ups. At this stage, highlights and hot spots can be added to increase depth and give the green a wet look. I decided to leave white out of the final step, thus giving the piece a dark, eerie look. I've seen many pieces ruined by too many highlights and last-minute touches. Remember, when it comes to highlights, less is more.

8 Strip off all the tape, then add a slight drop shadow to the edge for a floating-off-the-surface illusion. While this design can be used as a stand-alone mural on a tank or hood, it's also a good effect to include in a graphic or on a T-shirt to attract attention. The final step is to apply a clear coat of HoK UFC-40 urethane. The clear coat not only protects the surface, but also adds a whole new dimension of depth that is impossible to obtain with non-cleared surfaces. Besides penetrating the layers of urethane tones, the clear reactivates and brightens the colors and acts as a light transport to provide that "reach-in-with-your-arm" depth that custom automotive paint jobs are known for.

Paint naked!

CHAPTER 17

SKULLDUGGERY

1 Though skulls are fairly simple to render (none of those pesky eyes or facial wrinkles to deal with), it's still handy to have a model to sketch from. And skulls make great conversation pieces. The entire design is sketched in white chalk on a black basecoated sign blank.

2 Using HoK opaque white, follow the preliminary sketch with a standard 0.3 mm Iwata HP-C. Because the background is black and all of the colors are transparent, it's important to provide a base for all the white details first so that they will be visible later.

3 Since skulls have no skin or musculature, they are void of expression. Although this vacant stare can be quite effective, sometimes a bit of artistic license must be taken to provide character. Using a metal straight edge the horizon line of the cemetery is sprayed in.

Now, what would an F/X book be without a few skulls in a lonely cemetery? Although this "skull landscape" is closer to the lines of a mural, it's not dissimilar from graphics. Today, graphics are barely discernible from murals with their complex fades, details, and airbrushed goodies. I especially like using skulls and silhouetted landscapes of cemeteries or boothill-style horizon lines for graphics filler or background work. (This, of course, depends on the style of the car.)

Even if you've never had the desire to paint a hood mural, I can guarantee you will eventually be asked to put a few skulls on something. So for all you "kitty kat" pillow airbrushers out there, grit your teeth and try something new.

4 Examples can be seen in the art of such masters as Michael Whelan and Frank Frazetta. In this design, I chose to have a pile of skulls receding into the background, with a cemetery backdrop.

5 With a mixture of Cobalt Blue and Oriental Blue Kandy, begin to shade and bring out the image of the skulls. Though the entire design may appear to be blue at this point, you must remember that this is a color-layering process and that the majority of the blue is merely a base for the next color.

MATERIALS & EQUIPMENT

3M masking tape
White chalk
Skull Master shield (optional)
Metal ruler or straight edge shield
House of Kolor (HoK) Basecoat White
 BC-26
HoK Basecoat Black BC-25
HoK Oriental Blue Kandy Koncentrate
 KK-4
HoK Cobalt Blue Kandy Koncetrate
 KK-5
HoK Violette Kandy Koncentrate KK-17
HoK Intercoat Clear SG-100
HoK Reducer RU-311
Iwata HP-C .2, and .3 mm top-feed
 airbrush
Iwata RG-2 touch-up gun
Iwata Micron-C detail airbrush

6 As in the previous demo, use transparent basecoat black to punch up the details and add depth to the shadows. Due to the back lighting from the moon, black is also used in this piece to define the horizon line and the tombstones in the background. It is also used in the details of the rifles and the cracks In the skulls

7 As in the previous demo, use transparent basecoat black to punch up the details and add depth to the shadows. Due to the back lighting from the moon, black is also used in this piece to define the horizon line and the tombstones in the background. It is also used in the details of the rifles and the cracks In the skulls

Paint to live, live to paint skulls!

8 Using opaque white and the Micron airbrush, brush in the detailed highlights and brighten up the lightning in the background. White is also used to give the horizon line, tombstones, and surrounding clouds added depth.

9 With the majority of the design complete, the smoking bullet holes, blood, and glowing eyes are added. The finishing touches can make or break a piece. I love to hide things in the details—a picture within a picture. Not all of my hood murals suggest the macabre. These hidden details and embedded signature have become my trademark and major selling point.

CHAPTER 18

THE ART OF SKULLING

(NO, NOT THE BOAT THING...)

Where would the kustom paint business be without the art of airbrushing skulls? The previous chapter covered the freehand technique of skull airbrushing. Another alternative to the joy of skull painting is the use of moveable mask and freehand stencils. Gabe McCubbin commissioned me to design a series of skull stencils for novice and expert airbrushers. The result is the Craig Fraser Skullmaster series recently released by Artool/Medea.

I highly encourage the use of freehand shield systems. I use them often because they provide a softer edge than masking tape and a cleaner, harder edge than you can get from freehanding, without the fear of overworking the area. I first learned about freehand shield systems from Radu Veru's *Complete Studio Handbook,* which, in my opinion, is the finest airbrush book ever written. You can order it through *Airbrush Action* magazine; I highly recommend it! I've been making these stencils/shields for the past 10 years out of anything from acetate to photopaper, even X-ray film. Artool has saved me a lot of X-Acto cutting and layout work by making a number of shield shapes available. Not to mention how much more convenient it is to have a shield that is urethane-proof. So if you're a purist, and you feel that shields are evil, don't knock it until you've tried it!

1 Pictured here are a passel of Freehand Shields to play with. These particular shields are from Artool. The series is the new Skullmaster designed by yours truly.

2 These stencils are identical. Soak overnight in lacquer thinner and the one on the left will look as new as the one on the right. Before using any commercial or homemade stencil, be sure it's solvent-proof. All it takes is a little solvent to convert an ordinary stencil into a potato chip!

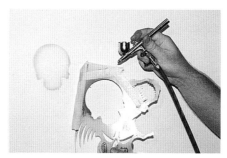

3 Mix a batch of HoK Violette Kandy. Using the Frontal Skull stencil, spray the positive element of the skull outline with the Iwata Eclipse-C. Be careful not to brush the stencil across the wet paint when lifting it, otherwise you'll smear your work. (Not a good thing!)

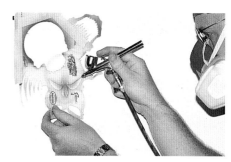

4 Choosing the evil eyes on the stencil, position and spray the eye and nose area. If you were to choose the normal eyes on this particular stencil, you would mask off the second set of eyes. The masking is important, since overspray can wreak real havoc when working with stencils.

5 Move the stencil back into position to align with the positive area already sprayed, and lightly fog in the gum line for the teeth. The bottom edge of the teeth was already laid out with the positive area. The image of the stencil in front of you can play a nasty negative/positive game on your perception!

6 After removing the stencil, you can see how the image starts to take shape. Use the small crack design in the Screaming Skull stencil to spray in a crack in the head. Though the three skulls in the pack are separate entities, you can use them together quite often.

7 Sorry, for those of you who thought there was only going to be stencil work; it's time to freehand! Freehand sketching with the airbrush not only softens the mask lines, but adds a lot more depth. In this case, you should add a drop shadow and some streaks running underneath the skull image.

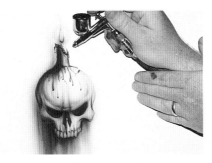

8 Just to be different, go ahead and add a melted candle on top of the skull. By incorporating more and more freehand airbrushing into the piece it becomes difficult to differentiate the stencil areas from the freehand areas. (This, of course, is the point.)

9 Switching over to white basecoat, apply slight highlights to the skull to punch it out more. Because of the white basecoat on the panel, the effect is not as dramatic in this demo. Your highlights will only stand out as much as the contrast of the surroundings will allow. A little highlight in the center of the eye sockets adds a ghoulish touch.

10 Using the same stencil, create a similar skull with the alternative eye design. This eye design is the classic blank stare look, reserved for most skulls. (Usually the angry eyes are reserved for characters that have skin.)

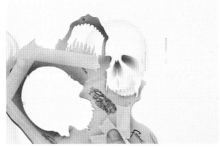

11 With the lower jaw section of the stencil, add a different bottom jaw to this skull. Note the masking tape throughout the stencil. This masking tape is necessary to prevent overspray into the surrounding pattern areas.

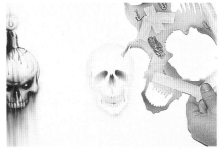

12 Here you can see the negative and positive elements of the lower jaw in the stencil. By repositioning the lower jaw, you can also alter the opening of the mouth itself. Pretty cool, huh? To simplify the design, have the mouth shut for this one.

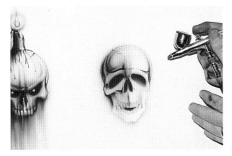

13 Using freehand, shade and shadow the contours of the skull to give it shape and depth. As in this case, you can give a hard horizon reflection to the skull to give it a polished or chrome effect.

14 As you can see, the freehand airbrushing of the skull is a necessity to complete the image. The stencil acts merely as a template for the completed image. A faded spiral surrounding the skull ads a "twilight zone" touch to the image.

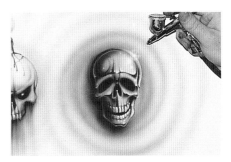

15 Using HoK White Basecoat, punch out the highlights and emphasize the light source. The highlights add a nice touch to the chrome effect. Normally you would use a multiple-color rendering for chrome, but the point comes across in monochrome.

16 For the third skull, switch to the side profile Screaming Skull stencil. The side profile skull has the jaw already attached, as can be seen in the positive relief airbrushed on the board.

17 Use the same stencil for the crack as was used on the first skull. On this stencil, as with the others, there is a selection of circles and half circles for the eyes, just in case you want your skulls to have a little more personality.

18 More freehand! Again, this is necessary to give the skull realistic depth and to cover the unnatural shield edge of the design. Good freehand skills will dramatically improve your overall work, so practice as much as you can. Plus, it's fun!

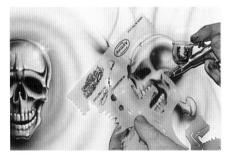

19 Using the negative section of the stencil, sharpen the edge of the teeth and redefine the positive image. You can also try adding a few freehand flames into the background just to change the design a little. (Sorry, I can't help it. It must be a design defect of mine).

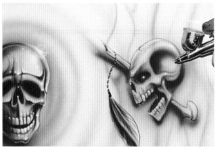

20 That darn design defect of mine again! By throwing in a single bone and a feather attached, the skull suddenly takes on a native American look. Any design should be allowed to progress as you paint. If you stop the creativity of your work at the sketching phase, you'll bore yourself to death (and usually your audience).

21 With the third stencil, The Multiple, you can add a background design of spiraling mini skulls. Again, it's important to mask off the specific skull that you want to spray.

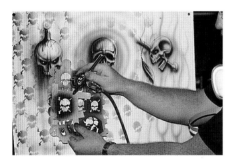

22 Switching to the skull and crossbones stencil, add another pattern to the first skull design. This type of close patterning is pretty cool, because it takes on a dual image. From a distance, it looks like a paisley pattern; the skulls only appear as you approach the image. This is a great automotive attribute.

23 The part of the Multiple stencil that I've used the most is the section with the "screamy faces." They're little screaming faces, some with hands, some without. They're quite effective when combined with a flame or smoke effect in a mural. They also make great graphic filler.

24 While there are a number of other applications for these Skullmaster stencils, this panel demonstrates a good sampling of some of the things that you can do with them.

25 Here's a good example of how you can use the Frontal Skull stencil without freehanding (for those of you who don't want to practice!) The job was a 40-foot trailer for West Coast Choppers. The trailer was to have the two devil logos and Maltese crosses on both sides, as well as tribal flames covering the length of the sides and back. After spraying the flames, and before unmasking them, I decided to airbrush a fade at the tips and an entire background of skulls. I airbrushed the positive of the skull first. This was the fastest way to establish a pattern for the entire design.

26 After covering the entire flame design with skull outlines, I then complete the skulls by focusing the airbrush in the center between the eyes. This made it quite fast (which counts when there are about a thousand skulls to paint....thank goodness I got my prototype stencils that week!) I used three identical stencils for this, since I had to rotate whenever the stencils got too wet and loaded with paint.

In this chapter, you learned how to use stencils and freehand airbrushing to complete the design. The trailer is a good example of how these stencils work without freehand and how they can save quite a bit of time and sanity! It's important to realize that no stencil system is a magic wand. Stencils are merely tools. They can be under-used and over-used. But when properly used, they can improve the overall design, and shave time off any job.

For all you skullaholics, keep an eye out for the sequel..."Son of Skullmaster" Stencil Series. Soon to be lurking at your neighborhood airbrush shop!

Superskullifragilisticexpiallidocious!

27 On the jacket of the devil, I added a little stencil pattern of the West Coast Chopper logo. This duplicates the original "Coop" artwork that Jesse James used for his logo. I cut this stencil out of the back of a 4" x 6" photograph. Since the jackets did not require too many crosses, the photo technique worked out fine.

28 Here is the completed piece. (Actually the flames are still waiting for their drop shadow and final pinstripe. After this is done, the whole trailer will be clearcoated.)

MATERIALS & EQUIPMENT

3M masking tape
Artool Skull Master stencil set
House of Kolor (HoK) Violette Kandy
   Koncentrate KK-17
HoK Intercoat Clear SG-100
HoK reducer RU-311
Iwata HP-C top-feed airbrush
Iwata Micron-C airbrush

CHAPTER 19

HOMAGE POUR GIGER

Although the biomechanical style has become popular recently among many automotive artists, few give credit to the originator, H. R. Giger, who pioneered this macabre blend of the living and the mechanical. He is the innovator and Oscar award-winning genius behind the movies *Alien* and *Species*. Giger has done for the macabre and gothic art of this century what H.P. Lovecraft did for literature. Giger's dark fantasy art is disturbing in many ways, but most disquieting is his blending of recognizable objects and anatomy in a way no one would ever see in reality. (At least one would hope never to see!)

You can interpret another artist's style without copying it. Giger pioneered the biomechanical style, but not the gothic undertones and influence that he used to create it. Always try to expand a style and experiment to bring something of your own to the design. While I used a number of reference pieces from Giger's book series *The Necronomicon* (available through *Airbrush Action* magazine), I also added quite a bit of my own goodies to give it a unique twist.

Biomechanical not only makes a nice mural style, but a great background landscape piece too, as in the demo of Jason Whitfield's CRX street racer (Chapter 20) . Give it a try; it won't bite. (Maybe.)

1 Sand the surface of your powder-coated sign blank with 600-grit sandpaper, then mask off the border. (For those of you who have ignored the first 18 chapters. Ha! Ha!) To obtain a metallic look, spray the sign blank with HoK Orion Silver Shimrin using the Iwata RG-2 gun with the fan tip.

2 Using one of Giger's art books, or other reference material, sketch the rough design using white construction chalk. When rendering a biomechanical design, try to maintain balance in the layout with implied symmetry. If you study Giger's work, it has balance; yet, when observed closely, it has no true mirror-image symmetry. To quote Giger, "Symmetry is a sign of insanity."

3 Using a weak (over-reduced and transparent) mixture of black urethane toner, begin laying in the rough outline of the design using masking tape and straight edges to give faint but sharp edges to the border. For this demo, I used a masked-off circle template to airbrush rivets and screwheads with the bottom-feed Iwata Eclipse. The transparent black allows the silver to show through, giving the black a ghost image.

4 Using a movable mask cut from photo paper, I defined the random images before freehanding the details. Although I used a Giger book as reference, the design is an interpretation of Giger's biomechanical style and not a duplication of an existing image. You can learn more from an artist by breaking down and analyzing his style than by just copying an image. (And your neck doesn't hurt so much from looking back and forth at the book!)

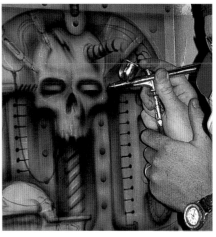

5 Setting aside the freehand shield, I switched to the top-feed Iwata HP-C to start freehanding in the details. This is the fun part. Just let your imagination go. Keeping yourself in the same biomechanical mindset, be sure to step back and look at the work often to make sure you're not overworking or crowding a particular area.

6 When the majority of the image is laid out, go over the whole surface lightly with a worn red Scotch-Brite pad and water. Not only does this knock off any high spots and eliminate overspray, but it also removes the last of the chalklines. Be sure to scuff the surface in only one direction so that, should you accidentally scratch the mural, the metal will have a damaged or aged look. (Heck, you might want to scratch it on purpose!)

7 Using the 0.2-mm HP-C detail gun and the same mixture of HoK black toner, finish the details and make the background recede by darkening it and casting shadows. The transparent toner is perfect for shadowing and can become opaque by layering.

8 A trick to use whenever working on small panels or shirts is to turn the design upside down when finishing the detail. This is helpful for reaching the lower areas and will improve the balance of the final design by tricking your brain into seeing it as a group of shapes and not your intended design. (Of course, this doesn't work when airbrushing on cars!)

9 Switching to a combination of HoK Tangerine and Root Beer Kandy Koncentrate, create a red oxide kandy and use it to airbrush a rust pallor and water damage streaks into the design. This not only breaks up the monotony of the black and silver but adds overall depth to the piece. Plus, it gives it a sickly, neglected look.

10 After removing the tape border, use the Micron-C for the razorfine highlights along the metal edges. Hot spots are also added to the skull and curved surfaces to emphasize the light source and shadows. Note the added rust streaks and the drop shadow on the bottom right of the image in the photo. Even though this is just a demo piece, this gives it a framed 3-D touch.

11 The result: a good conversation piece for anyone's portfolio. This high-profile biomechanical style can be tied in with graphics as a background landscape or as a stand-alone mural for any Harley, hood, or jacket mural.

As you can see, it's not as difficult as you'd think. It just takes a little patience and, like all the demos in this book, a little practice. The cool thing about the biomechanical style is that once you get the hang of it, you can improvise. This keeps up interest when you've got a large area to paint. I like to hide little things in the mural for the owner or show judges to find. Kind of like a twisted "Where's Waldo?" game.

Rest in Paint!

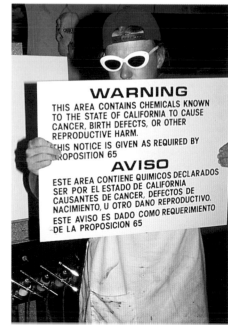

12 One final note—if you have a hard time coming up with metal sign blanks for painting, I recommend using those pesky "urethane warning" signs that tend to clutter up the paint shop. With a piece of sandpaper, all that "hazardous material" writing comes right off! (Just kidding! I couldn't resist leaving this one in there. The OSHA guys gave me such a hard time about it when it appeared originally in a magazine article.)

MATERIALS & EQUIPMENT

3M masking tape
X-Acto knife
White chalk
3M red Scotch-Brite pad
H.R. Giger reference books or a good
  biomechanical reference art piece
A very macabre mood
House of Kolor (HoK) Orion Silver
  Basecoat BC-02
HoK Black Basecoat BC-25
HoK Tangerine Kandy Koncentrate KK-8
HoK Root Beer Kandy Koncentrate KK-7
HoK Reducer RU-311
HoK White Basecoat BC-26
Iwata HP-C top-feed airbrush
Iwata RG-2 touch-up gun
Iwata Micron-C top-feed airbrush
Iwata Eclipse bottom-feed airbrush
Circle template
Photo paper for random freehand
  shielding

Two sides of a Kawasaki ZIR Motorcycle tank. The entire bike was a biomechanical nightmare.

CHAPTER 20

KILLING TIME
"PAINTIN' A 10-SECOND HONDA"

The best thing about kustom painting is that you never know what's going to come through your shop door at any given time. A few years ago, I wouldn't have believed that a Honda CRX could race a quarter-mile in under 12 seconds, let alone that we would be painting one that would make it in 10! This was a 10-second, 1.5 liter, intercooled, turbo-charged, nitrous-sucking, street-killing Honda. As soon as we found out that this machine was coming from Shawn Carlson's Newformz shop, the paint job was a must. Shawn's penchant for larger than life intercoolers, and his habit of making stock drivers hit the sound barrier, was a painting opportunity we couldn't pass up. We decided that if we could go half as crazy on the graphics as he normally does on the powerplant, we would have one show-stopping paint job. Plus, Hondas are small and don't take a lot of work. (Right!)

Shawn and his partner, Jason Whitfield, the car's owner, didn't let us down. Not only was this Honda full tilt, the whole thing was attached by Zeus fasteners just like a racecar. This seemed cool at first, until the little Honda expanded to fill our shop with about a dozen or so panels, and every little chrome Zeus retainer needed to be masked! Needless to say, Jason wanted a conservative race-boy paint job at first, some checkers, a few scallops (zzzzzz). Most street racers pride themselves on their conservative paint jobs, in contrast to the out-of-control engine under the hood. Luckily, we had our yellow Toyota truck, "The Last Look," in the showroom that day. After staring at it for about an hour, Jason changed his mind and told us to make his paint job as radical as possible. We were to do whatever we wanted, as long as it was the ultimate.

We called up our buddy Vern Cantwell at Valspar/House of Kolor, and with a firm cover deal for *Turbo Magazine* (Shawn Carlson is also an editor for *Turbo*), we worked out a sponsorship deal. After a few meetings and half-a-dozen concept renderings, we were ready to begin. Since the Honda was going to destroy any previous quarter-mile time records for a car in its class, we decided to name it "Killing Time." With the deadline only a few weeks away, the clock was already ticking.

1 With the body fairly well straightened out and the base color already applied by our buddy Shawn Carlson, Dave did some last minute body-blocking and prep work before the graphics were applied. He used 600-grit wet/dry sandpaper to knock down the shine and pre-cleaner to remove any fingerprints or other contaminants from the surface.

2 After finishing the prep work, K-Daddy laid out the primary body graphic with 1/8" 3M blue fineline tape. (K has been using this brand of tape for years due to its clean-edge characteristics, ease of turning, and repositionability. And, when laying out graphics, there is a lot of repositioning, believe me!) K likes leaving the kustom rims on the vehicle when painting. As he's said many times, "How can you get into laying out the graphics when you're looking at a pair of ugly steel rims?!" Of course, they're covered up when spraying.

3 Since we used the base color of the Honda as an integral graphic in the design, K laid it out first and surrounded it in 3M masking tape. This area remained masked throughout the entire graphics process. With the primary green area masked, he then laid out the first series of colors to be sprayed with the same 1/8" blue vinyl tape. This initial layout is much like a sketching process, where the design is modified and overlapped areas are determined before the masking paper is applied.

4 Mixing a batch of HoK Passion Pearl Shimrin, K-Daddy sprayed the first color using his gravity-feed Iwata LPH-100 spray gun. The low overspray characteristics of the Iwata HVLP spray gun allowed K to get good coverage on the graphics without having to fully mask the entire car. (This saves tape and paper expenses, not to mention labor.) You can just make out my rendering under the tape on the hood. K used my design for the initial layout and from there, it became a free-for-all.

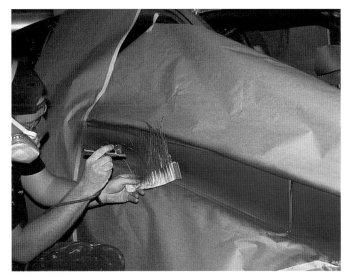

5 After K-Daddy sprays the Passion Pearl graphic, I use the Wisk Broom stencil (which is literally the strands of a wisk broom cut off and taped together, proving you can make interesting stencils out of anything. Of course, it renders a perfectly good broom useless in the process) and spray in a random pattern using Candy Burple.

6 Because K-Daddy staggered the colors sprayed, he was able to use his patented "back-masking" technique and spray the next color with only a 15-minute drying window. This technique allows him to spray up to 5 colors in one day with limited masking on each of the color surfaces. Of course the HoK basecoat urethane's fast drying times don't hurt either!

7 Using a mixture of HoK Tru-Blue Shimrin and Cobalt KBC Kandy Basecoat Koncentrate, K-Daddy sprayed the second color. Unlike other kandy blues, K doesn't base in white first, but sprays the color over the existing green. The addition of the Shimrin designer pearl to the KBC Kandy creates a color opaque enough to cover without allowing the green to bleed through. This again saves time and eliminates the high tape edge that results from multiple-stage painting.

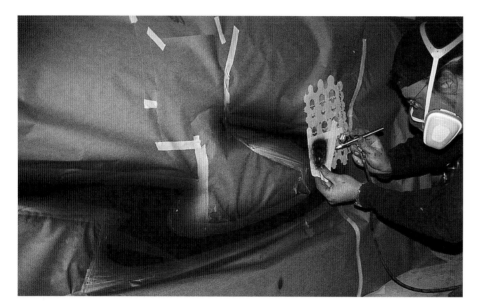

8 Giving the paint about 15 minutes to dry, I used my Iwata HP-C top-feed to add some stencil designs to the graphic with a mixture of Cobalt Blue Kandy intensifier, SG-100 Intercoat clear, and Violet dry pearl. The blue blends into the base, but the pearl gives the stencil designs punch when viewed at certain angles. The stencil used here is one of the three new Skull Master series I designed for Artool.

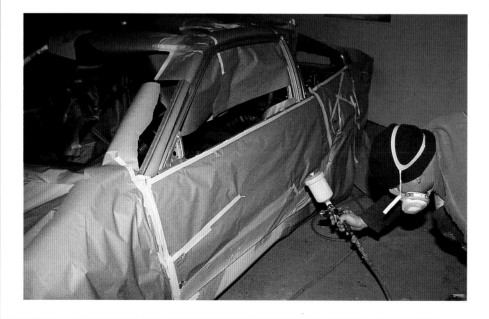

9 K masked and sprayed the yellow graphic using a combination of HoK SG 101 and 102. Since yellow is notorious for bad coverage, he used a light base of BC-26 White before spraying.

10 Sneaking in again between colors, I added a little life to the plain yellow with some varied streaks of HoK Tangerine and Root Beer Kandy combined with lavender and orange dry pearl. The lavender pearl gives a bright red reflection to the orange tint when the light strikes it. Dion refers to this touch as the "fire effect," a favorite trick on our yellow graphics.

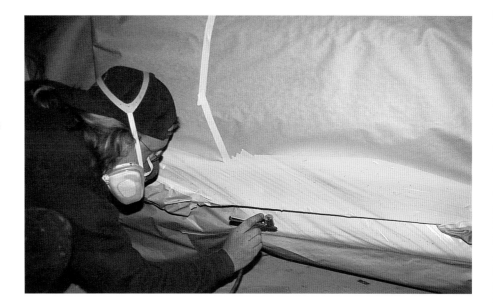

11 Proceeding along with the concept in his head (I usually give a rough draft of the colors in the rendering, but K-Daddy has the final word on the layout), K laid out and sprayed a Kandy KBC Magenta and Persimmon pearl graphic. Notice the respirator K and I are wearing throughout the painting process. Whenever spraying any paint, whether it be urethane or waterbase, always have adequate ventilation and respirator protection. We definitely prefer using a booth and a dual-cartridge respirator everyday versus lung problems.

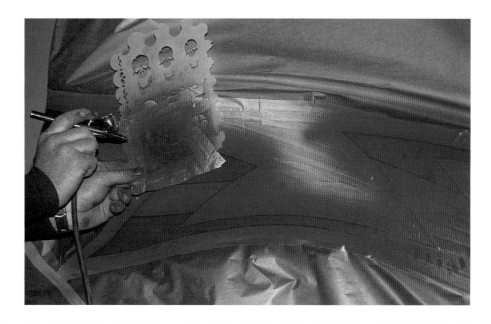

12 Using a different section of the same skull stencil, I airbrushed a pattern of the "screamy faces" (remember them?) onto the graphics surface. To create a ghosting effect, I used the same Kandy Magenta that K used, but added blue-pink interference dry pearl. This causes the color to shift as you walk around the car, and even sports a slight fluorescent effect when viewed under certain exterior lighting at night.

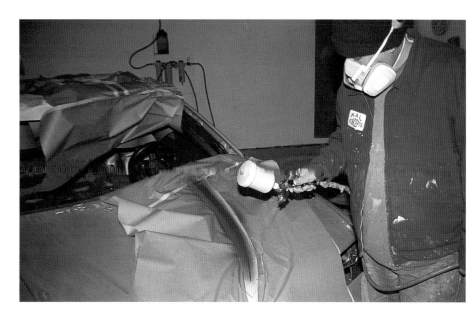

13 Instead of basecoating the Kandy Organic Green, K combined the white directly in the mix to increase its coverage and soften the green by dropping the color value a few notches. This was the last color change of the day for K-Daddy. He then allowed the designs to dry overnight before masking on top of them for the final layouts.

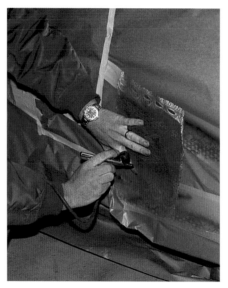

14 Finally, I sprayed a slightly more labor-intensive pattern in the graphic, using a blue/green pearl in the Green Kandy. Jason Whitfield had wanted a paint job as radical as the motor in the car! For this effect, I got some lace material from the local fabric store. By spraying repositionable adhesive on the back, I was able to lay it against the surface and spray through it without having it shift around.

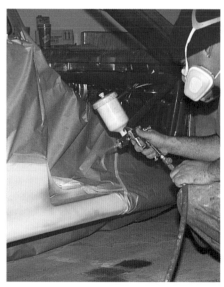

15 One of the graphics K-Daddy usually lays out last is the checker pattern. This is because it's one of the most time-consuming. By laying the others out first, you can usually get away with masking off less area in the long run. The first step is the white, which must be given at least an hour to dry before masking over. (This really messes up K-Daddy's speed-masking deal.)

16 With 1½" masking tape, K-Daddy laid in a crosshatched pattern, which he alternated to make the areas that needed cutting easy to see. This trick eliminates the need for drawing cutting lines since the tape acts as its own guide. (Another one of K-Daddy's patented speed-masking techniques.)

17 With all the checkers cut and peeled, K sprayed in a coat of BC-25 Black. After giving this time to dry, he found Dave and let him have all the fun of peeling the remaining masked checkers.

18 After Dave double-checked for any leftover tape scraps and uneven checkers (there's nothing worse than finishing a graphics job only to peel off a bit of tape in the middle of a four-color fade), I used a mixture of Violette KBC Kandy with Purple Haze pearl and airbrushed in some streaks. This not only added some color to the checkered area, but gave the surface an undulating flag-like appearance.

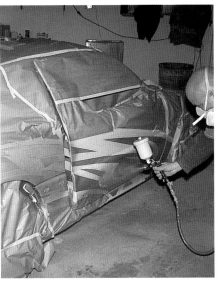

19 After the checkers dry, the entire graphic job is remasked, leaving only the original background color of the Honda exposed. This final graphic is actually the background to the graphics themselves.

20 K-Daddy prefers a neutral gray or silver as a background color. This makes the graphics stand out without competing with the primary color of the vehicle. Some colors don't play well with others. Silver is a good equalizer.

21 Instead of the standard marblizer effects we usually do in the backgrounds, I decided to give Jason a little something extra (well, actually, he also was willing to pay a little something extra): a Giger-type biomechanical landscape covering the whole background. This design was entirely rendered in a weak solution of over-reduced black with a bit of silver to tie it in. The silver also pulls a double duty of giving the image a slight ghosting quality.

22 After the two-day ordeal on the background, the entire body was unmasked and a streaked effect was added along the edge of the original green (a mixture of Kandy Organic Green Intensifier, Intercoat clear, and lime pearl) bordering the graphics. Using the same streaking style, the name of the car, "Killing Time" was rendered across the hood. (To the careful observer, it is also seen across the back bumper, underlying the crisscrossing graphics.)

23 Ron Beam performed the final striping, which he applied with HoK striping urethane. The final green he used on the primary graphic is a special concoction of neons and standard colors that look fluorescent, and even glow a bit under black lights, but don't have the fading characteristics of standard neons.

24 With the pinstriping completed, I applied the last of the touch-ups, highlights, and hotspots. These were applied using an over-reduced transparent white and my Iwata .2m HP-C detail gun. Hotspots, tracers, highlights, whatever you want to call them, are not only indispensable for hiding small flaws and "paint boogers," but also add a unique touch, or as some people say, a "swoosh," to the graphics.

25 Just when I thought I had seen the last of the biomechanical nightmare of the paint job, Dion and K-Daddy brought out the nitrous bottles, seat, and helmet to paint. Oh well, at least I didn't have to sit on the concrete to paint them. As a final touch to all of the biomechanical landscaping, I added a fade of HoK Purple/Orange Kameleon. Over-reduced and sprayed through an airbrush, the Kameleon takes on a whole new characteristic as a tinting system. You can still see all of the biomechanical details, but as you walk around them, they have a radical color shift from purple to blue to orange. Though the Kameleon is pricey (about $450 a quart), compared to standard paint, it gives an effect not achievable by any other pearl system...and I only used about 2 ounces of it throughout all of the background fades.

26 With the touch-ups and everything else completed, the Honda was given a final precleaner/tack rag wipe down; then, Dion rolled it into the booth for the clearcoat. Using his favorite gravity-feed, the LPH-100 "secret weapon" by Iwata, Dion gave the Honda and all its new graphic goodies a tack coat and three good wet coats of Valspar AC-2135 polyurethane clear. After the car was sanded, Dion gave her one more session and she was off to the buffers, then back to Newformz to be assembled in time for the *Turbo* magazine cover shoot and the Battle of the Imports finals in Anaheim.

And there is a good example of a typical Kal Koncepts/Air Syndicate week (a year-long project we had to complete in 9 days...but we're not complaining.) Street racers are not only demanding of their powerplants, but also of the individuality of the paint job; and this is one set of paintworks that is as loud, and as fast, as what's under the hood. Similar in many respects to the previous graphics demo, "Killing Time" had a few more goodies added to it. The airbrushing alone pushed it into the "radical" category of West Coast Kustom Paint!

In Paint We Trust!

MATERIALS & EQUIPMENT

3/4", 1", and 2" 3M masking tape
1/8" 3M blue fineline tape
36" 3M masking paper
X-Acto knife or razor blades
600-grit 3M wet/dry sandpaper
House of Kolor (HoK) Iru Blue Shimrin Basecoat PBC-36
HoK White Basecoat BC-26
HoK Black Basecoat BC-25
HoK Intercoat Clear SG-100
HoK Neutral Marblizer MB-00
HoK assorted dry pearls
HoK Blue-Red Kameleon Basecoat KF-08
HoK Passion Pearl Shimrin Basecoat
HoK Lemon Yellow SG-101
HoK Hot Pink Pearl Shimrin PBC-39
HoK Limetime Pearl Shimrin PBC-38
HoK Orion Silver Basecoat BC-02
HoK Violette Kandy Koncentrate KK-17
HoK Oriental Blue Kandy Koncentrate KK-4
HoK Cobalt Blue Kandy Koncentrate KK-5
HoK Organic Green Kandy Koncentrate KK-9
HoK Magenta Kandy Koncentrate KK-16
HoK Reducer RU-311
HoK striping urethane
Valspar AC-2135 urethane clear
Iwata HP-C top-feed airbrush
Iwata LPH-100 HVLP spray gun.
Artool Freehand Shields
Artool Skullmaster shields

CHAPTER 21

THE DRAGON'S TALE

The significance of the hood mural in automotive airbrushing is largely due to the fantasy murals that dominated the kustom vehicles of the 1970s. Influences like Von Franco, Bob Beam, The Wizard, and the Great Zacko can be seen in the work of many of the new airbrush artists who are taking automotive murals to the next level. While the styles and techniques of this new generation of automotive artists vary as much as those of their predecessors, they all have one thing in common: the desire to paint on a vehicle instead of a canvas.

The barbarian, or warrior, motif was one of the most popular subjects of automotive fantasy artists of the '70s. This genre was inspired primarily by the styles of Frank Frazetta and Boris Vallejo. Today's fantasy muralist is inspired by the likes of Michael Whelan, Chris Achilleos, Julie Bell, Luis Royo, Simon Bisley, and many others. These current influences have helped to increase the stylized quality of fantasy art.

While the hood mural in this demo smacks of the Frazetta-based masterpieces of the `70s, it is more of a hybrid than a reproduction.

Every inch of the '95 Dodge Neon was kandied with HoK Persimmon Kandy over a gold base with gold micro-sequins. (Whatever we didn't paint, the owner had gold plated.) Even the sides and door jambs are full of graphics interfacing with a continuous mural scene that extends around the entire bottom quarter panels of the body. The fenderwells, gas tank, and undersides of the car are muraled as well (I know, I need therapy). Since the theme of the Dodge is Dragon-oriented, with landscapes of fighting dragons bumper to bumper, the owner wanted a fitting name, "The Dragon's Tale." For this demo, we'll focus on the hood mural and after it's done, you'll see the rest.

1 After wet-sanding the hood with 3M 600-grit sandpaper, the entire surface is wiped with PPG DX-330 precleaner in preparation for the layout. Using a piece of white blackboard chalk, the initial design and massing study is laid out. The rough sketch acts as a framework to ensure balance and will be filled in and detailed as the mural progresses. Chalk is easy to wipe off, cleans up with water, and leaves no residue. I used a combination of reference books the client had already pored over.

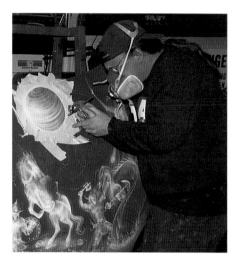

2 Using HoK Basecoat White, I continue the sketching process and build up the base details using my Iwata HP-C airbrush. 3/4-inch 3M masking tape is used to give the planet a clean edge. Everything else is free-handed.

3 Since the majority of the colors used in this mural are transparent kandies, it is necessary to use a white base to build upon. This stage is the longest, since many of the design's concepts and details must be decided upon before progressing to the first colors.

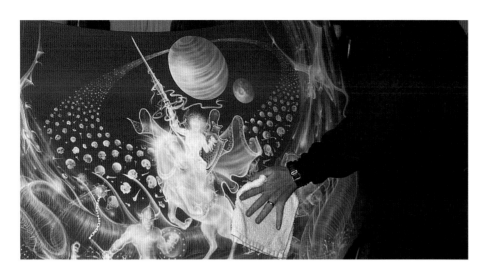

4 After the base design is finished, the entire surface is scuffed with a red Scotch-Brite pad and water. This not only removes the excess overspray, but also knocks down any high spots that can cause problems later when layering colors. After going back and touching up any scratches caused by the Scotch-Brite, the surface is again wiped down with DX-330.

5 Working from light to dark on the spectrum, I mix some HoK SG-102 Chrome Yellow and airbrush in all of the fire effects and areas that are primarily based in yellow, or reflecting the light of the fire itself. To give the yellow some extra reflectivity and vibrancy, I add a little HoK Screaming Yellow and Silver Dry Pearl. Though it's hard to see the difference while airbrushing, the pearls definitely stand out when cleared. (Notice the respirator mask that I'm wearing. When spraying urethanes, catalyzed or not—these are not—a good dual-cartridge respirator rated for organic vapors is a must.)

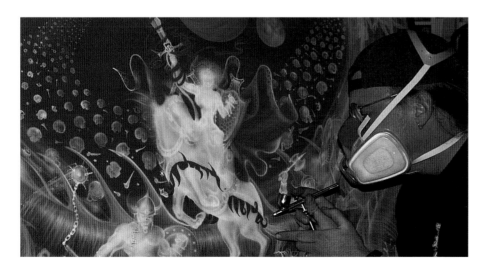

6 Using HoK Magenta Kandy Basecoat with a little Lavender Dry Pearl, I airbrush in the atmospheric streaks in the large planet and fill in the color of the girl's cape. An advantage to airbrushing with these urethane toners is that their high level of transparency prevents any overspray from muddying up the background Persimmon Kandy. If it wasn't for the white basecoat, the magenta would probably not show up at all.

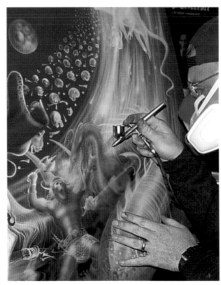

7 Mixing Cobalt Blue and Oriental Blue Kandy Koncentrate with Lazuli Blue Pearl, I continue the color layering onto the two skeletal warriors and the surrounding water area. (After all, what's a barbarian fantasy mural without skeletal warriors?) It's important to build detail as you progress in the color process, otherwise you will lose the vibrancy of your colors through overspray fogging, and your final detail and depth of field will also suffer. Since these colors are transparent, they're not too good at hiding mistakes later on.

8 After applying a small amount of the previous blue toner over the yellow, I decided that a true green was needed over the yellows of the fighting dragons to stand out, or they would appear too dark. With a combination of Kandy Organic Green toner, and Blue/Green pearl, I begin detailing and defining the musculature of the two smaller dragons.

9 With an even mixture of Tangerine Kandy Koncentrate and Root Beer, I create a transparent red oxide to color the tips of the flames, as well as the flying dragons. This red oxide is also used for the saddle leather, the large dragon's tail, and some of the creases and shadows of the green dragons. When sprayed over green, a sickly brown results, giving the dragons a dingy, weathered appearance.

10 One of the most versatile colors in this mural, Deep Violet is used to airbrush in the details of the horse's harness and the warriors' battle clothing. It is also used to darken the shadows and features of the large dragon tail emerging from the water behind the horse. This is the first major color used without a dry pearl added to it because of the potential clogging problem when using a fine detail gun.

11 The transparent violet is also used as a detailer over the green dragons. By using these progressively darkening colors to create light and shadow, the use of black is massively reduced. This not only saves time, but also gives the mural more vibrancy by having little actual black to stop the transport of light in the clearcoated image.

 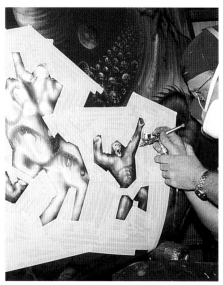 

12 With the background and detailing completed, return to the foreground and the three main characters. Using Incredible White Mask liquid frisket, outline the characters and mask off their armor, clothing, and jewelry. Being ammonia-waterbased, the liquid mask dries quickly and is best applied with the included applicator nib or a lettering brush. (Don't use your favorite brush for this, or it will more than likely be ruined by the latex.) I like this masking system because it doesn't give the edge of the masked area a knife-cut look.

13 After outlining the characters with liquid frisket, 3/4" masking tape is used to continue masking the surrounding area. This not only saves time, but when the masking tape is pulled off later, it helps pull up the dried fluid mask. To redefine the edges of the three warriors and horse against the background, a light coat of white is misted over the existing airbrushing—again with no pearl, since I want the edge to be subtle and not stand out too much after it's clearcoated.

14 With a little Cobalt Blue Kandy Koncentrate, I re-sculpt the musculature, this time with no pearl. These steps may appear redundant and the cause of paint build-up, but very little paint is used and, in the long run, the underlying details will show through after the final clearcoat, adding depth and muscle texture. Remember, the previous layer of blue included pearl, which adds depth and amplifies light, even when viewed through the non-pearled layers.

 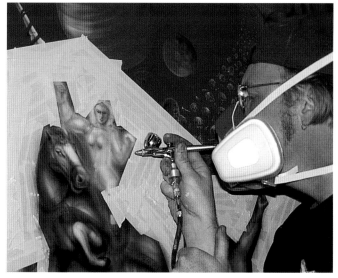

15 I want the horse to be grey, but I don't want to kill the color transitions of the piece by throwing in a monochromatic character. To solve this problem, I combine a transparent toner with some weak black toner. This not only allows me to shade and build depth with the horse along the grey scale, it also ties in the surrounding colors with the transition violet color. A freehand shield allows me to create sharp contrasts without the unnatural edge that tape can give.

16 Mixing a flesh tone from basecoat white, yellow, scarlet, and a few drops of blue, I base out the skin of the warrior. Since I'm going to come back and build up the muscles and shadows using red oxide, I want to make sure that the actual skin base is a good neutral flesh tone. If it's too yellow, it will appear orange, blue, or white, and she'll contrast too sharply with the vibrant colors around her. Remember, skin tone varies according to the surrounding environment and light sources.

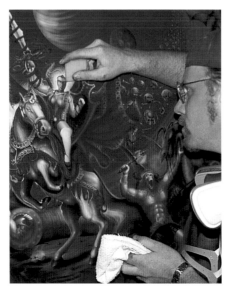

17 After giving her green eyes and scarlet lips, I continue the shading and sculpting with an over-reduced deep violet toner. Again, this transition violet will not only tie in the surrounding elements of the mural to the girl, but when used over a properly blended flesh tone, will result in a natural brown that tones down the orange from the red oxide. To use black at this stage will kill the image, and wipe out all of the transparent layering that's been rendered up to this point.

18 With the masking tape removed, use a small rubber eraser (included in the Incredible White Mask kit) to rub off any excess masking. This eraser doesn't damage the urethane basecoats, but lifts up any leftover latex buried by the color layering. (When airbrushing water-based media, be careful with this technique; it can literally erase your airbrushing.) I also use a damp towel with a small amount of precleaner to pick up any stray eraser particles or smears.

19 Using HoK Blue Blood, I airbrush the individual strands of hair using the Micron-C detail gun. Different layers of Tangerine Kandy and Violette are also sprayed in to build depth and define the shadowed areas of her hair. The Blue Blood color is also over-reduced and fogged over various areas of her body to create a blush effect and used on her lips for an added highlight.

20 With the primary airbrushing completed, it's time to lay in the gold and silver leafing used on the warrior's outfits and weaponry. Since the sizing (glue) that is used to adhere the leaf is susceptible to precleaners, I wait until nearing the end of the mural to apply it. The sizing I used is the solvent-based One Shot quick-size, and was applied using a #1 and #2 lettering quill. It's important to remember that the edge of your gold or silver leaf is only as good as the edge you brush on. Taking time at this stage can save you hours of touch-ups later.

21 After letting the sizing set for about one hour, I test the area by touching it with the back of my finger. If the sizing is still tacky, but doesn't come off on my skin, it's ready for the leafing. Using the tissue backing that separates the individual sheets of leaf in the book, I gently press on the leaf, slightly burnishing it through the tissue. I'm not being too careful at this stage to keep the wrinkles out of the metal, since they add a sense of character and detail to the jewelry and weapons, giving them a rough-hewn metal appearance.

22 Giving the sizing an hour to dry, the excess leafing material is brushed away leaving the brushed-on image behind. Using transparent cobalt blue, red oxide, and violet respectively, I airbrush in the shades and shadows of the leafed areas, tying them in with the surrounding mural. By using actual metal leaf in this way, I can create reflective base colors that not only look like metal swords and helmets, but that reflect light in the same way that the actual objects would.

23 Besides using the airbrush to create the details of the leafed weaponry, it is also an indispensable tool for softening the edges of the previously masked and leafed areas. When the airbrushed foreground characters are complete, they not only blend in with their surroundings, but stand out as well, giving the overall mural more of a 3-D illusion.

24 With all of the colors completed, last minute touch-ups and highlights remain. Using over-reduced HoK Basecoat White Shimrin, the final highlights and hotspots are dispatched again using the Micron-C for the hair-fine detailing. While hotspots can make a piece, they can also break it. When adding final touches to anything, the adage "Less is more" applies again.

MATERIALS & EQUIPMENT

3M masking tape
Incredible White Mask
X-Aacto Knife
Circle templates
Artool Freehand Shields
White Chalk
House of Kolor (HoK) White Basecoat
   BC-26
HoK Black Basecoat BC-25
Hok Chrome Yellow Basecoat SG-102
HoK Intercoat Clear SG-100
HoK assorted dry pearls
HoK Oriental Blue Kandy Koncentrate
   KK-4
HoK Magenta Kandy Koncentrate KK-16
HoK Violette Kandy Koncentrate KK-17
HoK Tangerine Kandy Koncentrate KK-8
HoK Root Beer Kandy Koncentrate KK-7
HoK reducer RU-311
HoK Blue Blood Shimrin Basecoat
   SG-105
Rolco quick size glue
Composite Gold and Silver leaf
#1, 3 Mack lettering quill
Iwata HP-C top-feed airbrush
Iwata Micron-C airbrush
Iwata Eclispe bottom-feed airbrush
Valspar AC-2135 urethane clear

Well, there it is—the cure to the common paint job. Although hood murals may not be for everyone (many people don't even consider them a legitimate art form), this same quality is what makes them so popular in the tight circle of automotive kustomizing. With automotive airbrushing and fantasy art on an upswing, the Kustom Kulture has never had it so good. There are few good airbrush artists out there, and even less who would commit their work to a hood or Harley tank. This subculture mentality is exactly what fuels the field and prevents it from becoming saturated. Automotive airbrushing is ever-growing and never dull. So dust off your airbrush, crack open your favorite fantasy book, crank up the Boston, and have a little fun.

Paint to Live, Live to Mural!

CHAPTER 22

A HELMET FOR ALL OCCASIONS

(THE FLAMED-OUT BRAIN BUCKET)

1 Disassemble the helmet, mask off the underside, and sand the black gelcoated surface with 220-grit sandpaper. It's necessary to sand and reseal the gelcoat due to mold-release waxes in the gelcoat that can reactivate later, causing lifting or bubbling of the clear if not sealed properly.

3 Giving the primer a few hours to fully dry, K-Daddy sprays on a combination of HoK Orion Silver Basecoat and HoK Solar Gold. This base gives the Kandy Apple a deep metallic look. (You can tell how long ago this how-to was shot...K-Daddy still had hair!)

2 After sanding the entire surface, K-Daddy sprays it with a catalyzed polyester sealer. This sealer/primer locks in the mold-release waxes and gives a good sandable foundation for the upcoming paint. Any nicks or scratches are taken care of at this stage with a catalyzed polyester filler.

4 Notice the slight gold shimmer of the metallic. The gold is necessary in the painting of a true Kandy Apple paint job. The gold lessens the brightness of the red kandy and gives it a richer glow than if it was solely shot with a silver base.

One of the fastest growing fields in kustomizing is the after-market helmet-painting industry. Ranging from motorcycles and Indy cars to sports like hockey and cycling, the market for individualized helmets has doubled in the past few years. If you have a little motivation and a well-ventilated garage, you can make a sizable dent in this industry.

Helmets range from $100 to over $1,000 for a kustom Kevlar Formula helmet, and the cost of kustomizing is fairly high too. Although many helmet owners are happy with their factory sticker kits, nothing is quite as expressive as a custom painted helmet. In all of the motorsports arenas, the rider is considered practically naked if he's not sporting a full-blown custom painted helmet. (Of course, his sponsors like them too, especially when their names are plastered all over them!) This market has grown so large that many automotive painters and airbrush artists have begun specializing solely in spraying helmets.

For this demo, I picked a rather simple helmet so the process was not lost in all the airbrush tricks. This particular helmet was done for Steve Stillwell, the editor of *Hot Bike* magazine. Steve wanted something unique on his brain bucket. He wanted it to be a classic design, but also wanted to have some airbrushing in it too. The helmet also had to match the kandy color of his bike and the flames. Nothing like a little challenge.

The helmet we used is known in the industry as a half-helmet or beenie. Be aware that beenies aren't legal in all states.

Although Steve's helmet was used, even brand-new helmets should be prepped, which involves removing stickers on or under the gelcoat clear. For durability and quality of finish, we use only urethane-based products. From prep to airbrush to final clearcoat, this job was completed using only the finest HoK and PPG urethane products. Since we switched all our paint systems to HoK and Valspar, I've modified the text so it's up to date with our current shop standards.

5 Starting with a tack coat first, K-Daddy dusts the plate and helmet with HoK UK-11 catalyzed Kandy Red. The tack coat provides an important tooth for the subsequent wet coats to adhere to. Without the tack coat, it's quite common for any additional coats to run, especially on curved surfaces such as this helmet.

6 After applying three additional wet coats of kandy, the true color of the helmet begins to show through. It's important not to give the helmet too many coats of kandy; besides the obvious running and sagging problem, the kandy will also continue to darken. A true kandy will darken until it appears black. This may be desirable for some effects, but not if you're trying to match a lighter shade of kandy already on the bike!

7 A protective coat of clear is applied after the previous color coat. Then let the helmet set for 24 hours before sanding in preparation for the airbrush work. Using 600-grit wet/dry sandpaper, knock down the shine to provide a good surface to work on. The design is then lightly sketched using pure white chalk. This is the same inert chalk that I use for all my design work. It wipes off easily and leaves no residue to interfere with the clearcoat.

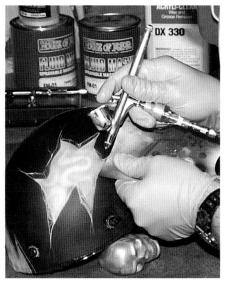

8 With HoK Basecoat White, I continue the sketching process using an airbrush. The brains and breaks in the helmet are retraced and detailed over the chalk sketch. (The nitride rubber gloves are great for artists who are sensitive to reducers. Personally, I feel claustrophobic with them, so this is the only demo where you'll see me wearing them.) (Of course, the aluminum skull support for the helmet is an absolute necessity.)

9 After finishing the white, I wipe the entire surface with a damp rag and precleaner. This removes any of the excess chalk as well as overspray. I do this wipe-down process after every color change, giving me a clean surface for every step, and preventing the build-up of dry areas caused by overspray.

10 Donning my superman gloves, I came back to battle crime with some HoK SG-101 Lemon Yellow Basecoat. An Artool Freehand Shield allowed me to control the overspray and give the area a sharp, soft edge without the buildup that a taped edge would give—not to mention that the freehand shield is a heck of a lot faster and leaves no tape residue.

11 Next, build up the detail using a mixture of Tangerine, Root Beer, and Pagan Gold Kandy Koncentrates mixed with intercoat clear. The result is a transparent red-oxide that works nicely in sculpting the brains (disgusting, huh?).

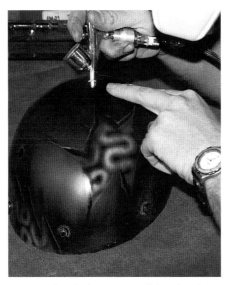

12 The darkest areas of the details were done with a mixture of transparent Violette and Cobalt Blue Kandy Koncentrate and intercoat clear. This creates a deep purple color that appears as red/brown when layered over the red-oxide and yellow. Continuous layering gives the illusion of black in the detail without killing any of the colors.

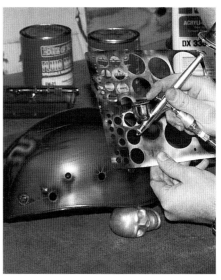

13 To create the realistic bullet holes in the sides, I use an architectural circle template. The purple kandy mixture is used with a few drops of black added to it. The black makes the bullet holes stand out from the details in the brains and give them more depth.

14 Last, but not least, the highlights and rising smoke from the holes is airbrushed in white. To get the extra fine detail in the broken edged highlights and thin wisps, I used the Iwata Micron-C airbrush. The white is even further reduced to prevent spitting and clogging at this detail range.

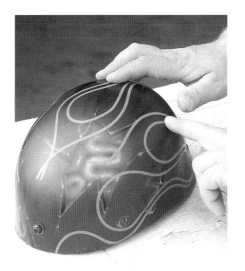

15 With the airbrushing done, the helmet is given a light coat of clear to protect from the masking. Non-catalyzed intercoat clear is used because it has a drying window of only one hour. The surface is then scuffed to prepare for the flame layout. The flames are laid out using 1/8" blue fineline tape. Fineline tape is perfect for helmets since it can turn a radius without bunching, and is repositionable.

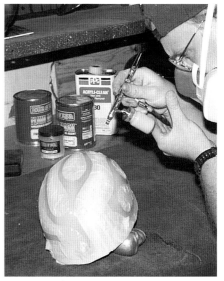

16 After the blue fineline tape is applied, mask up to the edge with 3/4" masking tape to cover the surrounding area of the shell. With the previous batch of SG-101 Lemon Yellow Basecoat, paint the flames with the Eclipse airbrush. The Eclipse not only has a wider spray pattern, but the bottle allows me to spray longer without refills.

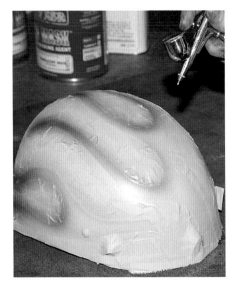

17 Mixing up more of the red oxide concoction, spray a light orange fade on the tips of the flames. A little Lavender Dry Pearl added to the Red-Oxide Kandy gives a deep red color when layered over the yellow.

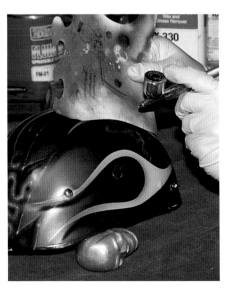

18 After the tape is removed and the surface is wiped down with pre-cleaner again (tape residual), use a free-hand shield to help lay in the drop shadows under the flames. The drop shadow is sprayed using a transparent over-reduced mixture of Basecoat Black.

19 Then, switch to an Xcaliber 000 sword striper brush. With a little HoK Lite Blue urethane striping paint, carefully pull a line around the flames. Practicing striping on an old helmet is an excellent way to build up brush control and mastery.

20 The helmet is then taken into the booth and clearcoated. Dion uses his trusty Iwata LPH-95 to lay down a tack coat and three good wet coats of HoK UFC-35 Komply Klear. While a helmet normally needs one final clearing session, this one may need to be sanded and cleared again to eliminate the pinstripe edge. K-Daddy also sneaks in the driving lights from his 1955 Ford. (The eyeball paint scheme is a rare factory option.)

Clearcoated, polished, and reassembled, this helmet is ready to ship back to Stillwell in time for the "Loveride." While motorcycles may be more impressive to paint, it's nice to know that for every bike you paint (at least in California), there must be at least one helmet to go along with it. Always offer the customer a deal—a matching helmet at half price if it's done at the same time as his bike. Limited only by your imagination and the size of your client's wallet, a custom painted helmet is definitely an original way of dealing with the current helmet laws.

Although the techniques covered in this chapter were applied to a little peanut helmet, remember that ninety percent of all helmets are made in the same manner, with gelcoat skins. These same techniques also apply to hockey helmets, baseball helmets, Nascar helmets, skiing helmets, and even bicycle helmets. While they may not fetch as high a price as the hood murals or full-blown paint jobs, there are many more of them, and you'd be surprised at how many airbrushers are making a pretty good living dressing them up!

Late-Air!

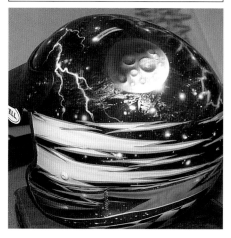

MATERIALS & EQUIPMENT

3M masking tape
3M 1/8" blue fineline tape
3M 220 and 600-grit wet/dry sand-
   paper
White chalk
House of Kolor (HoK) Basecoat White
   BC-26
HoK Black Basecoat BC-25
HoK Kandy Apple Red UK-11
HoK KC-10 Wax & Grease Remover
HoK Orion Silver Basecoat BC-02
HoK UFC-35 Urethane Clear
HoK Reducer RU-311
HoK Tangerine & Rootbeer Kandy
   Koncentrate KK-7, KK-8
HoK Chrome Yellow SG-102
HoK striping urethanes
X-Caliber 000 striping brush
Iwata LPH-95 HVLP spraygun
Iwata HP-C top-feed airbrush
Iwata Micron-C airbrush
Iwata Eclipse bottom-feed airbrush

CHAPTER 23

THE REAR WINDOW

With car clubs on the rise, there is also an increased demand for club logo designs. Although many companies specialize in producing vinyl logos, a new trend based on the old school hand-lettered style is gaining popularity. While not a huge market, quality club windows consistently draw prices from $100 and up. A fast painter can easily earn $300 to $500 per day painting window murals.

Since many clubs compete with one another, club logos are an important part of car shows. They give the clubs recognition and can have a positive impact on points during judging. Although there are many different techniques for painting windows, here are the steps that work for me in delivering both speed and quality.

Initially, I give clients three to six concepts from which to choose from. I then enlarge the chosen design to the size and proportion of the average window, usually 14" x 42" (this can be done freehand or with a projector), and transfer it to a sheet of 3M masking paper. When I'm happy with the layout, I re-sketch my pencil design with a black Sharpie pen to make the lines easier to read and to get a better idea of the overall layout.

One particular club, Art of Noize, has been on the southern California truckin' scene for quite a while. Previously known for their vinyl windows, the club members wanted something a little more individualized to attract more attention.

When all final changes were made and the members were happy with the new window style, I retraced the design using a pounce wheel. This tool allows me to create tiny perforations along the lines of the image and transfer the design onto the window using either the airbrush or a bag of chalk. After pouncing a design, it's a good idea to hold up the stencil to the light to make sure no lines were missed. (For individual windows that are not to be duplicated, you can save time by freehanding the window instead of making a stencil.)

1 A clean window is the best canvas. Although a window may appear clean, always wipe it down with an ammonia-based cleaner and then a precleaner/de-waxer. This eliminates any wax build-up or water-beading that may affect the adhesion of the paint.

2 After positioning the stencil on the window, I go over the entire design with a pounce bag. The bag I use is really just a knotted shop rag filled with blue construction chalk. I like the blue chalk because it's easier to see, and it sticks to the glass better than talc. Red chalk is good too, but I find it has a tendency to discolor the paint.

3 After carefully removing the paper, you'll see a faint but readable line through the pounced pattern. With this method, you'll be able to make dozens of windows from one stencil. Before painting it's important to blow off any excess chalk dust (even the blue chalk may discolor your lighter colors).

MATERIALS & EQUIPMENT

3M masking tape
3M 36" masking paper
Pounce wheel
Pounce pad and chalk
One Shot sign enamels
#1,2,4,6 Mack lettering quills
Smoothie fish-eye eliminator
One Shot low temp reducer
Xcaliber 000 Sword Striper
HoK Kandy Organic Green
  Basecoat KK-9

4 Using a #6 lettering brush and One Shot lettering enamel, I brush in the main body of the lettering using metallic silver. This gives a reflective base to the window design and makes it stand out more at night when headlights shine on it. Though it's possible to use the enamel right out of the can, I prefer to add some medium temperature reducer and a few drops of Smoothie. The reducer speeds up drying time, while the Smoothy prevents fisheyes and eliminates most brush strokes from the surface.

5 Mixing a batch of emerald green and white, brush in Oriental slash style lettering along the bottom of the design. When working on a window, I like to jump around from area to area while allowing certain elements to dry. This not only saves time, but also prevents having to work over a wet area. Although I don't use one in this demo, a mahl stick, or even a ruler, can be used to keep your arm off the surface when painting.

6 With the Iwata HP-C, begin airbrushing in the background skull landscape in the lettering. Though the majority of the window is One Shot, I used HoK Kandy Organic Green intensifier (HoK KBC Kandy Green Basecoat works well, too) for the airbrushing. The reason for this is the high transparency of the HoK urethanes, and the fact that they airbrush a little cleaner than the One Shot. Since the urethanes may react to the One Shot and cause lifting, it's important to use very small amounts, and not to build up a wet coat. This kandy green is also used to shade the bottom letters, giving them a little more character.

7 Going back to One Shot white, brush in the base for the skull and flying money. In these particular club windows, I tried to vary the individual cars by changing the colors and by adding different backgrounds and airbrush effects. This is the main advantage to hand-painted club logos. For this window, the owner wanted a money theme, so the "Z" in the standard Noize logo was changed to a "$" symbol and a devilish green skeleton was painted coming through the "O" with flying dollars clenched in its hands.

8 While letting the white set, I add some tinting black to the premixed white for a medium gray. Using this gray and a #4 lettering brush, I carefully brush in the drop shadow around the main lettering. This not only adds depth, but fills space in the design. Since the lettering is to be outlined, the edges do not have to be perfect.

9 Mixing a batch of lemon yellow One Shot, I outline the lettering using a #3 long quill brush (the longer the brush, the more paint it will hold for a continuous, even line). However, this is not important in this case, since I opted for a more stylized slashed and splattered line. I also added a drop of black to the yellow to help it cover better. I know it sounds weird, but it's an old Pinhead trick and, trust me, it works.

10 Using the airbrush with transparent green toner, begin filling in the details of the green money devil. (Note the little green dollar signs in the background letters and the pupils of the skull. It's the little details that they talk about.) Again, be careful with the urethane on the enamel. If the enamel is too dry and you put a wet coat of urethane on it, it will lift up. If the enamel is too fresh, you will get a crackled finish in your urethane airbrushing. (Unless of course you want that look.)

11 With the green airbrushing finished, switch to One Shot black. By adding some tinting to the enamel, I'm able to get a semi-transparent black that is excellent for rendering details and shading. Still using the HP-C, tighten up the details and add drop shadows to the skull figure and flying money.

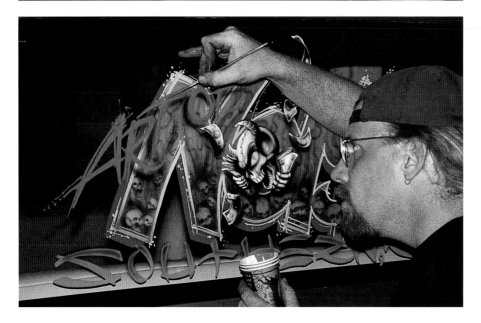

12 Using a medium green, add "Art of" to the logo. Staying with the splattered dry-brush look, I also come in with the same black in the airbrush and add a drop shadow to help the letters punch out. Normally, I like to jump around the color wheel when painting, but since the truck was Del Sol green, and the theme was money, I decided to stay in this spectrum.

13 Switching to a higher value, I mix some aqua One Shot to add a thin highlight to the darker green lettering. This not only adds more color to the design, but will make it easier to read from a distance. Whenever possible, I avoid custom mixing and try to stay within the standard colors offered by One Shot. (I try, but I'm not always successful.) This makes it easier to match the previous colors for later touch-ups.

14 Thinning down some One Shot white with medium temp reducer, I put the final highlights and hotspots on the finished piece. It's best to do these final touches after the paint has had a little time to set, or the pressure from the airbrush can move the fresh paint around, causing lifting problems later.

15 The result: a window that should attract a lot of attention for the club, and hopefully future work for the airbrush artist. (Don't feel shy about adding your signature and phone number to a finished piece, just don't make it too obvious or obnoxious.) This design took approximately 1-½ to 2 hours to complete (the work goes faster if you paint on more than one at a time) and cost about $140. The time and price vary depending on the amount of detail and airbrushing. It's up to you.

Stay Painted!

CHAPTER 24

THE CLEARING GAME

In the kustom painting field, there's probably nothing less appreciated and yet as important as the clearcoat. Clearcoating is not just a good idea—it's a necessity. Since 99 percent of all show-quality graphic jobs are two-stage basecoat urethanes, it's a safe bet that after the artwork is done, the final piece is clearcoated. While many people may not consider spraying clear to be an art form, I guarantee that after trying to clear something yourself, your attitude will change. There is a phrase in the industry: "Behind every good clearcoater, there's a better buffer." Though this may be true in some circles, clearcoating remains an art form that is easily completed, yet rarely mastered.

This chapter focuses on urethane clearcoating. Although there are a number of synthetic enamel, lacquer-based, and even water-based urethane clears floating around, the bad boys on the block are the solvent-based polymers, known as acrylic urethanes and urethane enamels. Recent urethanes are taking advantage of the most current innovations in polymer technology. As far as clearcoating goes, I'm a good airbrusher, so I usually leave the clearcoating to my partners in crime, Dion and K-Daddy.

WHAT IS CLEAR?

In automotive painting, a clearcoat is a protective coating sprayed over the basecoat. This not only protects and seals the paint from the elements, but gives the final paint job its overall gloss and deep shine. All automotive final clearcoats are categorized as catalyzed clear. In the acrylic urethane field, these clears use an isocyanate-based catalyst to harden the clear much like the catalyst in epoxy cement hardens the resin. When the catalyst is mixed with the urethane resins and reducing solvents, the chemical reaction causes heat, a necessary ingredient in the drying process. While all urethanes are toxic and require proper ventilation as well as respirators, iso-

With many quality high-solid urethane clears on the market, sometimes the choice comes down to personal preference and availability. Here are a few that we use at Kal Koncepts/Air Syndicate.

Available in powdered or paste form, mica pearls, when added to the clearcoat, can add a spectrum of color and depth to your existing paint job. Some of the new interference/hologram pearls and metal flakes can cause a color shift and the 3-D illusion of depth in the paint.

cyanates are the main bad guys out there. Isocyanates are a nerve toxin and require the use of professional respirators at all times. For complete protection from long-term exposure, the Occupational Health and Safety Administration (OSHA) recommends using fresh-air systems in the work environment whenever isocyanates are present.

The basecoat is the first stage of the two-stage system and the clearcoat is the second. Single-stage paint, used for single-color paint jobs, is any paint that has the clear already mixed in. A three- or four-stage system is used to describe a job that requires additional clearcoats—these either contain a mica-based pearlescence, an applied kandy, or a tinted clear that is shot over an existing metallic and then sprayed with a final coat of transparent clear to finish the job. The easiest way to spot multiple-stage paint jobs is by the illusion of depth in the color created by the number of coats of transparent kandies or clearcoats. The more layers of clear painted on a surface, the better the ability of the paint to trap, reflect, and amplify light. Metallic bases, metal flakes, and pearls can be added to give the clearcoat the ability to modify light. Because of the hardened resins and the high DOI factor (Distinctness of Image), urethane clears can be buffed and polished to a mirror-like finish, unlike the older modified alkyd enamel systems that, while sufficient at the time, had yellowing problems. Urethane clears are not only handy in the automotive field, but also when painting on guitars and other hard surfaces like carbon fiber, fiberglass, and even floors. Due to their flexible nature and UV absorbing factor, they've been experimented with on vinyl substrates as a sealer and as protective coating for airbrushed effects on vinyl.

A series of Iwata HVLP spray guns ranging from touch-up to medium-spray gravity-feed to large siphon-feed. Airbrushes and small gravity-feed touch-up guns do not fall into the HVLP catagory of full-sized spray guns. Since their percentage of material to the surface is actually higher than most of the full-size models, no modifications were necessary to make them environmentally legal.

HVLP AND OTHER ACRONYMS

The weapon of choice for today's hot-shot clearcoaters is the HVLP (High Volume Low Pressure) gun. Actually, in most states it's not just a good idea, it's the law according to the VOC boys (Volatile Organic Compounds.) These VOCs are a standard used to measure the amount of solvents and other airborne paint chemicals that atomize into the air when painting. These guns put out a higher volume of material with less overall nozzle pressure, resulting in less overspray waste and more material on the surface. Not only arc they more environmentally friendly, but they have also improvcd spray quality. Able to hold a wider, more even fan of material (up to 17" in some cases), these guns have a material transfer percentage of anywhere from 70- to 90-

percent compared to the 20- to 30-percent efficiency of the older siphon-feed, non-HVLP models.

HVLP spray guns come in both siphon-feed and gravity-feed models. Many professional painters prefer the gravity-feed sprayguns to the siphon, due to the higher-volume rate of flow and the added clearance under the gun (the color cup is mounted on top, which makes shooting car roofs a lot easier on the wrists). The automotive spray-gun, though appearing unchanged on its surface, has undergone more internal design changes in the last five years than it has in the last five decades. The number of gun manufacturers has increased as well. As with many of the top-of-the-line paints, it's a matter of personal preference as to which one is best. But remember, the gun doesn't make the artist, it just makes his job easier. As long as you stick with known brands such as Iwata, Binks, Sata, and DeVilbiss, you can't go wrong. But again, like paint, sometimes your local distributor will make the decision for you. After all, what good is the ultimate spraygun if you can't get any rebuild kits for it?

CLEARLY SPEAKING

In light of today's advanced chemical technology and improved urethane clearcoats, you would think that clearcoating would become simpler, as well as better. In actuality, it's becoming more complicated. With the advanced chemicals being developed to catalyze and dry the clears better, the clearing process is becoming more of a thinking man's game, rather than just something you spray out of your paint gun. Clearcoaters must now learn more about chemicals and reactive properties to understand the modified mixing ratios required and environments needed for the best clearcoats. Safety precautions are becoming more complicated as well. Clearcoats may be environmentally safer now, but they're more dangerous for people. I highly recommend taking one of the classes/workshops that individual paint manufacturers offer to credential painters for their paint lines. Besides catalyzed clears, there are a whole batch of air-dry clears that have become known as intercoats. These intermediary clears are distant cousins

Even though the clear may be fresh from the can, it's a good practice to run all material through a strainer before spraying. All it takes is one blotch of hardened resin to ruin your day. Also be sure to keep the cans sealed tight. Besides being the law, it prevents the clear from becoming contaminated by water vapor, which can cause urea crystals to form.

When clearcoating a graphic job or hood mural, Dion chooses between his gravity-feed LPH 94 and his siphon-feed LPH-95. Here he's using the siphon-feed, since he wants less material sprayed when laying the first wet coat on the hood. The gravity-feed has a higher flow rate and has a better reach for rooflines and under doorsills.

Though hand cleaning is probably the most effective method, it is also time consuming. No paint shop should be without a gun-washer. This is a top-gun model that uses airpowered cleaning solvent to spray on and through the guns, much as a dishwasher. (In many states, it's legally required.)

Bonding clear, adhesion promoter, and intercoat clears are necessary products. Because the new high-solid, low-reduced clears currently on the market are not as hot, the clears do not bite into the surface as hard and require adhesion promoters to prevent lifting and snake skinning.

to the old air-dry lacquers and are designed to be sprayed on between colors to protect from color bleeds, promote adhesion, or act as a fast-drying carrier for a pearl or kandy tint. Being air-dry, these interclears are still urethane-based and still require solvent for reducing, but since there's no catalyst involved, they don't have the structural integrity of the catalyzed clears and cannot be used as a topcoat. Because of their nonstructural strength, it's actually a good idea to limit the number of coats to four when spraying with them. Otherwise, there could be adhesion problems, as well as cracking.

While there are a number of books and paint articles defining the art of painting and clearing, probably the best advice is to experiment. (If you've read the previous chapters, you've noticed by now that I like this word.) Most clears that are illegal in your area will be unavailable; and, as far as mixing ratios go, labeling is usually pretty self-explanatory. The art is not in how to follow instructions, but how to modify them for your individual use. For example, since temperature is a major variable, the clearcoater's use of the proper reducer, as well as the proper amount, can have a great effect on the final finish of the piece. Take into account that the pressure at the gun, the possible use of an accelerator to increase drying, and the window between wet coats are all situations that can be followed in the instructions, but need to be experienced first-hand to be truly enjoyed (sorry I didn't mean to be sadistic).

To sum up, find an accomplished painter and pick his brain. I'm lucky to be able to yell my questions to Kal Koncepts next door and get answers from K-Daddy or Dion, who's a third generation car kustomizer. Granted, you don't have Kal Koncepts a stone's throw away, and that is why the first piece of equipment in your shop should be a telephone. I spent at least an hour on the phone with Pete Santini and Jon Kosmoski before writing this chapter (I edited out half the tech jargon, since it caused me to go into college chem-lab withdrawals).

YES GRASSHOPPER

Pete "when-you-can-take-this-paint-gun-from-my-hand, it-will-be-time-for-you-to-leave" Santini of Santini Paint of Westminster, California, is one of today's masters of clearcoating. He's been in the trenches as a second generation car painter and kustomizer and takes a practical approach to painting.

"Pick up a gun and start spraying," Pete suggests. "You can only learn so much from the tech manuals and seminars. You've gotta just get in the booth and start spraying. Until then, it's all academic. And it's not just a 9-to-5 job. You've got to be willing to stay the extra time to learn. When you're working, you can't expect the boss to let you just stand around and watch. When you go to college, no one pays you to learn, and it's the same way in the paint booth. The real learning takes place at 11:00 at night when you have a problem, you can't reclear it tomorrow, and you've got to make a decision."

Pete prefers to use a gravity-feed HVLP gun due to the higher volume of material it can move. "Today's guns not only spray more efficiently, but the higher atomization of the clear makes the new guns work better with today's clears. With the new clears having such a high solids content [amount of actual urethane resins that ends up in the finished clearcoat], you don't need to bury the work with multiple coats. Actually, too much of the new clears can end up giving a milky consistency to the finish."

According to Pete, there are currently problems in the industry. "It's a toss-up between the number of new products being thrown out on the market and the cost of materials today. When a major paint manufacturer has five new clears come out within three to five years, it's obvious they're using the painters as guinea pigs for research and development. These games may save the research industry money, but it makes it tough for the painters when a product is pulled from the market because it's defective. As kustom painters, we still have to guarantee the work."

Though primers may be the last thing people think of when clearing, the new flexible primers and flex-additives help the urethane paints and clears adhere to the flexible plastic body panels and bumpers on late model vehicles. (For all you environmentalists out there, don't freak out. I know some of these are now illegal. We were just cleaning out an old cabinet here.)

Many of the pearlesence and depth effects of our paint jobs at Kal Koncepts/Air Syndicate would not be possible with non-cleared single-stage paints. Peace, Love, and Isocyanate clears.

This problem is quite common in the industry, but can be seen as a direct result of competition between paint companies to put out the best product first. In defense of the paint companies, it's also a direct result of the constant changes in the environmental laws in a given area. While these laws do protect the environment to an extent, the beaurocracy pushes the paint costs to the point of bankruptcy for many painters.

"The average amount of materials to primer, paint, and clear a Camaro today run as high as $900. That same car would have cost less than $400 five years ago, the increase being in the paint and clear. The profit has got to come from the labor now. There's no room for profit in the materials for the painter," according to Pete.

The talents of a truly gifted clearcoater are not necessarily seen in the end product; a good buffer can fix runs, sags, and orange peel in the clear. A talented clearcoater not only saves materials but time by keeping these problems to a minimum. In an industry where labor and design innovation are the only profit center, only the talented can survive.

In addition to books and articles, videos are also available for automotive painters. Jon Kosmoski has had an automotive video series available for years, and at Kal Koncepts we have a three-video automotive painting and airbrushing series available through *Airbrush Action* magazine, as well as a new *Automotive Cheap Tricks and Special Effects* video to complement this book. Everyone should try clearcoating at least once, but for quality of finish and profit, hire a professional. Even if you have an in-house clearcoater, picking up a gun and spraying will give you an appreciation for the art and eventually make you a better automotive painter or airbrusher.

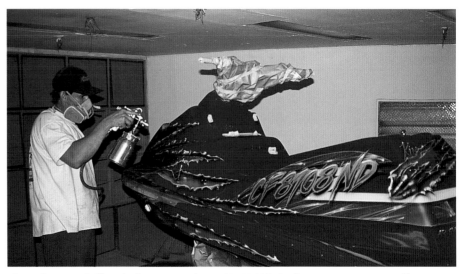

Certain specialized clears, such as HoK UC-1 clear, are an excellent choice for watercraft and racing applications due to their high quality shine as well as resistance to salt, fuels, and oils.

Whenever enamel pinstriping is involved, it's important to catalyze the enamel striping paint with the same catalyst being used in the urethane clear. Otherwise the clear can reactivate the enamel and cause lifting, as well as ribboning in the pinstripe.

One of the obvious points about clear is its toxicity. Respirators aren't just a good idea, they're a necessity. Here Dion has a little extra prevention going on while clearing this plane. By the looks of the clear cloud, I'd say it's a wise choice.

I don't care how "Johnny Bad-Ass" of a clearcoater you think you are, all clearcoats look better with a little buffin' and polishin'. K-daddy runs a wheel over the cured clear on the plane before its final reassembly.

The top polyurethane catalyzed clears out there can go over just about anything. Which is handy considering some of the varied products we use at KKAS. Just remember, all the products featured here are automotive-oriented. None of the paint warranties or factory support the urethane industries give for possible product failure apply if they are used over water-based textile paints. (Makes you think a bit, huh?)

IN CONCLUSION

While it's not possible to cover every aspect of a field, I've tried to address a large segment of the kustom painting industry that I've been a part of during the past decade. Regard these demos as a training system and springboard for developing your own style.

"Give a man a fish, and you've fed him for a day. Teach him how to fish, and you've fed him for a lifetime." In the kustom paint industry, the painter who is constantly growing and expanding his talents is the one who will survive. If you simply copy the demos, you may do well; but only in the short term. There are already plenty of faux Craig Frasers out there (which makes me feel good, but these painters will never be recognized as individuals in the industry, just knock-off artists). The techniques included here are for your basic knowledge. But by combining these effects with your own ideas, you'll develop a synthesized style uniquely yours. In today's competitive industry, where the equipment and materials are almost all of equal quality, individuality is all the kustom painter has. As I mentioned earlier, the demos in this book are not product-determinate. I've mentioned specific products because they're what I use. But nearly all of what I've done in this book can be duplicated using other equipment and quality brands of automotive urethane.

There are many new effects on the horizon. In fact, I've got a passel of goodies just waiting to break out at the next few car shows, not to mention the new kustom paintwork on Choppers that KKAS has been working on. To keep up with current trends, periodically check our website at www.gotpaint.com and keep reading *Airbrush Action*, and/or visit their website: www.airbrushaction.com.

Look for upcoming trends in the same places I do—magazines, television, movies, fashion, and art. Especially art. Art reflects society, but most importantly, if you interpret current art, then you'll have the upper hand in predicting the wants of the industry. Keep one foot in the past and one foot in the future and you'll do well. From reading this book, you'll see that a lot of the "Ol' School" techniques of the 1960s and '70s have resurfaced in modified versions, employing current technology and artistic tastes. Remember, there's no magic button, no secret mantra (sorry Zen fans). Just work hard, wear your respirator, eat your greens, and you'll be fine. As Ed "Big Daddy" Roth says, "Heck, if I can do it, anyone can!"

Paint to live, live to paint!

ABOUT THE AUTHOR

Craig Fraser operates the Air Syndicate airbrush studio in Bakersfield, California, and is the in-house airbrusher for Kal Koncepts. He is a contributing editor to *Airbrush Action* magazine and a freelance journalist for such publishing companies as MacMillan/Argus. Fraser is also a member of the Airbrush Getaway staff, teaching "Automotive Cheap Tricks and Special F/X." A spokesman and instructor for House of Kolor/Valspar and Medea/Iwata, Fraser balances his time between these jobs and his automotive "Kustom Kulture" Fine Art available through CoProNason. For more information, e-mail Kal Koncepts at fraser@gotpaint.com, or cruise the web site at www.gotpaint.com. For the internet challenged, you can always call the shop at (661) 836-3084.

GLOSSARY OF TERMS

Acrylic Urethane: A coating based on urethane chemistry that also includes acrylic chemistry as part of the cross-linked polymer backbone. (See urethane.)

Adhesion Promoter: Any additive that is sprayed onto a surface to create adhesion for a subsequent layer of paint or clear. Most adhesion promoters are sprayed onto surfaces that either cannot be sanded or are prone to lifting.

Basecoats: A two-stage paint system for automotive refinishing and kustom painting. The first stage consists of the application of the paint; the second stage is the necessary application of a clearcoat for protection and shine. All basecoat systems need a clearcoat without which they are dull and not U.V. protected.

Binder: The paint material that forms the film. So-called because it "binds" the pigment and any additives present into a solid durable film.

Buffing: A polishing technique used to remove sanding marks or surface imperfections.

Buffing Compound: A soft paste containing fine abrasives in a neutral medium. Used to eliminate fine scratches and polish the topcoat.

Catalyst: Any chemical used as an additive to catalyze (or stimulate a change) in a paint or clear system. A catalyst triggers a chemical chain reaction and causes the hardening of that paint or system. In automotive paint systems, catalysts usually consist of isocyanates or di-butyl tins that react with urethane resins.

Chroma: The level of saturation or intensity and richness of a color. Desaturated or "dirty" colors have less chroma while saturated or "clean" colors have more chroma.

Clearcoat: The protective urethane finish sprayed onto a completed automotive paint job. Clearcoats can either be a) "air-dry" clears, which combine with reducers and, when sprayed, dry by evaporation of the reducers, or b) "catalyzed" clears, which require a catalyst and a reducer solvent to harden. All finish clears on automotive vehicles are of the "catalyzed" variety.

Color Sanding: The sanding of a paint film to prepare for buffing or recoating.

D.O.I.: Distinctness of Image. A measurement of the accuracy of reflection in a paint film.

Drop Shadows: An airbrushed shadow beneath a graphic that gives the graphic a 3-D or floating illusion. Often used in lettering.

F/X or Effects: Term used to describe the airbrush or kustom-painted pattern or texture on a graphic or kustom mural.

Fish Eyes: A surface depression or crater in the wet paint film. Fish eyes are caused by repulsion of the wet paint by a surface contaminant such as oil or silicone. The depression may or may not reveal the surface under the paint.

Flake: A pigment consisting of flat reflective particles. Usually aluminum or metallic, providing special color effects to the final paint job.

Gold Leaf: Pounded gold sheets or a substitute composite material manufactured to appear as gold. The material is extremely thin and delicate, allowing it to conform to curved surfaces and be laminated onto vehicles for such techniques as lettering, striping, and mural details. Gold leaf is normally sold in books and can be purchased through most hobby stores or automotive paint/signage suppliers

Hologram Pearl: Often referred to as six- or eight-sided pearls, these are actually very finely ground hologram foils that shift through the color spectrum in up to eight different shades of color. Available only in a liquid form, hologram pearls are quite costly, usually starting at $450 for a sprayable quart. House of Kolor's line is known as Kameleon Kolors.

Hue: The colors we see such as: red, blue, green, yellow and all the shades in between.

HVLP (High Volume Low Pressure): An acronym used to describe a series of automotive spray guns. HVLP spray guns apply a high percentage (about 90%) of paint material to a surface with low levels of overspray, making them more economical and environmentally friendly than older versions. (Older sprayguns applied only 30-60% of the paint to the surface; the rest atomized and floated into the air as overspray). All licensed automotive body/paint shops in the U.S. are required by law to use HVLP spray guns. A spray gun's status as HVLP is determined by its volatile organic compound (V.O.C.), which is usually stated as a weight in pounds of non-exempt solvent per gallon of paint.

Intercoat: An air-dry clear used between painting stages or basecoats as a protective barrier.

Interference Pearl: Either a mica or foil substrate that acts with the same characteristics of a standard pearl, but casts two colors instead of the standard one (e.g.: blue/green, violet/blue). These pearls are used to create a shifting effect in the colors of the vehicle as you change your viewpoint to the surface. They are often referred to as "Flip-Flop."

Isocyanate: A hardening agent used with acrylic urethane and other two-component reaction type paints. It reacts with acrylic polymer, etc., to form a very durable coating.

Isopropyl Alcohol: An inexpensive, fast evaporating solvent, co-solvent or dilutant. Also called rubbing alcohol.

Kandy: A term used to describe the family of transparent colors used in automobile painting and kustomizing. The original term "kandy" derives from the "hard candy" look that the ol' school lacquers gave when layered multiple times. Today's kandies are predominantly urethane-based but still maintain this appearance when sprayed. These highly transparent paints are perfect for color process airbrushing and color layering in murals.

Kandy Koncentrates: A term coined by House of Kolor to name its line of Kandy Intensifier pigments. These Kandy Koncentrates or KKs are used either to intensify an existing basecoat system or in combination with intercoat clear for airbrushing. They are highly effective for airbrushing because of their very finely ground pigments.

Kewl: Internet and Kustom slang term for "cool."

Kustom: Anything that is modified from the original factory specs. When using kustom with a "K," the term refers to any art form or vehicle from the "hot rod" genre.

Kustom Kulture: Anything having to do with the art form or genre of the kustom hot rod or kustom car such as artwork, music, clothing, or actual vehicle kustomizations.

Lacquers: Paints that dry by evaporative loss of solvent. The film remains susceptible to attack by the same or similar solvents. Lacquers can be based on nitrocellulose or acrylic resins. For automotive applications,

these paints are illegal according to V.O.C. regulations in almost every state in the U.S.

Latex: An emulsion, usually a dispersion of a polymer in water. Often used in gloves or protective material. Also used as a liquid application masking system.

Lead: A metal commonly used in the manufacture of driers and pigments. Highly toxic, lead has been eliminated in a large number of automotive spray products.

Lettering Quill: A long-handled, short- quilled brush used specifically for lettering and touch-ups.

Liner: A long-handled, long-quilled lettering brush used for outlining letters and some striping applications.

Metallic Paint: Paint that contains metallic pigment, usually in the form of tiny flakes. Generally, these are aluminum or mica and are used to enhance the eye appeal of the finish.

Microencapsulation: The act of encasing certain chemicals in microspheres. Chemicals are released and activated only when the capsule in which they are encased dissolves (much like a time-release capsule used in medication). In waterborne systems, capsules remain intact, dissolving only when exposed to air.

N.A.C.E.: National Automotive and Collision Exposition. One of the largest collections of buyers, manufacturers, and distributors of collision repair and automotive repainting accessories in the world. This show is held once a year in different locations around the United States, usually in December.

Ol' School: In kustom painting, this term refers to any older method or

technique, e.g., the "ol' school" method of painting.

Orange Peel: An irregularity in the surface of a paint film, resulting from the inability of the wet film to "level out" after being applied. Orange peel appears as a characteristically uneven or dimpled surface to the eye, but usually feels smooth to the touch.

O.S.H.A.: Occupational Safety and Health Administration. Inquiries can be directed to OSHA, U.S. Department of Labor, Public Affairs Office, 200 Constitution Ave., Washington, DC 20210 or phone (202) 693-1999. You can also visit OSHA's web site at www.osha.gov.

Oxidation: A process involving the chemical combination of oxygen and the vehicle of a paint that leads to drying. Also, the destructive combination of oxygen with a dry paint film that leads to degradation or the destructive combination of oxygen and a metal (for example, rust).

Pearl: A mica substrate or any other substance used to add color or a metallic sheen to paint. Pearls come in a variety of colors and in dry, liquid, or paste consistencies. For airbrushing, the most popular form is the finely ground dry pearl. Pearls can be added directly to either the paint or the clearcoat. Their primary purpose is to create a secondary color cast to a paint job without affecting or diminishing the initial color of the vehicle.

Pigment: Small particles added to paint to influence such properties as color, corrosion resistance, mechanical strength, etc. Pigments may be colored, semitransparent, black, white, or colorless. They must be incorporated into a paint system by some dispersion process.

Polymers: Very large molecules built

up by the combination of many small molecules through a chemical process called polymerization. Polymers often consist of thousands of atoms, usually in chains or networks of repeating units.

Powder-Coat: A system of painting metal in which a powdered material is sprayed on the surface and then baked at 600°. The powder takes on the appearance of paint, but is much stronger. This system is similar to the ceramic glazing process, but power coating is performed at a lower temperature.

Powder-Paint: A similar technology to powder coating, but performed at a lower temperature —140°. This is a more practical method because it can be used on plastics, but it has less durability than powder-coating.

PPG: Pittsburgh Plate Glass Co., or more currently referred to as "Pittsburgh Paint & Glass," is one of the largest manufacturers of automotive paints and vehicle window glass.

Scotch-Brite: Spun plastic scouring pad manufactured by 3M and used for scuffing or light sanding duty. Scotch-Brite is available in different grits that vary according to color. Red Scotch-Brite is recommended for prepping a surface.

S.E.M.A.: (Specialty Equipment & Manufacturing Association): The largest after-market automotive product show in the United States, held annually in Las Vegas in November.

Semi Gloss: Usually a clearcoat that has neither a fully glossed nor a matte finish. Often referred to as a "satin" finish.

Silver Leaf: A pounded aluminum alloy that has many of the same characteristics as gold leaf, without the high cost.

Single-Stage: Refers to a type of catalyzed or air-dry painting system that needs no clearcoat, hence a "single-stage" application. These paints tend to be slow drying and, if they contain catalysts, are more toxic then the air-brush-friendly, two-stage basecoat systems.

Sizing: The glue used to adhere gold or silver leaf to a surface. Though there are a number of water-based sizings, the original solvent-based sizing is still the best for automotive and exterior signage applications.

Solvent/Reduce: A liquid that dissolves something, usually resins or other binder components. Commonly an organic liquid. In automotive applications: any type of petroleum-based reducer used specifically for thinning down or cleaning any solvent-based automotive paints or clears. The reducers are usually rated by temperature use or drying speed. The cleaning solvents are normally more caustic or fast evaporating.

Solvent Popping: Bumps or small craters that form on the paint film, caused by trapped solvent.

Squeegee: A rubber block used to wipe off wet sanded areas and to apply filler, putty, or vinyl application tapes.

Substrate: The object or material to be painted. It may be bare metal or an old finish.

Sword Striper: A type of short-handled, long-bristled brush used specifically for pinstriping. The name "sword" comes mainly from the sword/dagger look of the brush head.

Tack Coat: The first clear coat medium spray application, allowed to flash only until it is quite sticky. Also used as a protective coating to prevent reversion by the wet coat to the underlying surface.

Tail Solvent: A slow evaporating solvent that leaves the paint at a slow rate and allows the film to continue to flow and level. When trapped under layers of material from overapplication, tail solvents can cause solvent pop, or worse, delamination.

Thinner: Solvent added to a lacquer to reduce its viscosity to a sprayable consistency. (See solvent/reducer.)

Tint: An individual pigment from a family of pigments used on a mixing machine to produce a color match to the vehicle to be painted. Sometimes called tinting base or base system.

Toner: A reference to a base pigment system. (See Toner and Pigment.)

Touch-up Gun: Any small spray gun used to spray small areas, graphics, or door jambs in a vehicle. They are usually characterized by their small size and equally small spray pattern.

Two-Stage: Any automotive paint system that requires a second stage of clearcoating to seal and gloss the finish. (See basecoats.)

Urethane: A type of paint or polymer that results from the reaction of an isocyanate catalyst with a hydroxyl containing component. Urethanes are noted for their toughness and abrasion resistance. (See polyurethane.)

UV Inhibitor: Any additive to a paint or clearcoat which blocks the sun's damaging UV (ultra-violet) rays from penetrating the clear and either fading or oxidizing the underlying basecoat color. UV Inhibitors act much the same way as sunscreen.

UV Stabilizers: Chemicals added to paint to absorb the ultraviolet radiation present in sunlight. Ultraviolet radiation decomposes the polymer molecules in paint film and thus UV stabilizers are used to prolong paint life.

V.O.C. (Volatile Organic Compounds): The amount of material released into the atmosphere during paint spraying or product manufacturing. The V.O.C. regulation relates directly to the level of a chemical's toxicity and its ability to diffuse or break down in the atmosphere within a given amount of time.

Water-Based: Any paint or clear that is primarily water or uses water as a reducing element in its chemical make-up.

Waterborne: A type of paint that uses water as its primary carrier rather than typical solvents. This is not a water-based system, merely a carrier for a solvent-based, microencapsulated system.

Wet Sand: A technique involving the sanding of a surface while it is being flushed with water. This permits the smoothing of surface defects before subsequent coats are applied.

Zen: The unattainable level that everyone tries to achieve or acceptance that the well-traveled road to perfection is the true goal. In automotive kustomizing: observance and respect for what has come before, while still furthering one's own attempts. (This is Craig Fraser's description of Zen — any similarity to other existing forms of Zen is completely coincidental and absolutely unintentional.)

INDEX

THE ULTIMATE KUSTOM TRAINING
MASTER KUSTOM PAINTING IN 5 DAYS!
GET HANDS-ON TRAINING FROM WORLD-CLASS TALENT!

4-DAY CLASSES:

CRAIG FRASER'S KUSTOM MASTER SERIES
Pro use of stencil systems, realistic flames, airbrush techniques, ground metal painting, & much more! This class takes you to the next level.

PINSTRIPING & LETTERING MASTERY
Learn from legend Gary Jenson the materials, supplies, & skills to master pinstriping and lettering.

AUTOMOTIVE GRAPHICS
Learn the latest trends in auto kustom graphics, including flames, taping methods, complex designs, & much more.

AUTOMOTIVE MURALS ON STEEL
Kustom Masters Pantaleon, McCully, Soto & gang guide you through professional-caliber images, techniques, various texture effects, color use with HOK urethanes, & much more.

OTHER 4-DAY COURSES:
PIN-UP & CANVAS AIRBRUSHING
T-SHIRT AIRBRUSHING
COMMERCIAL ILLUSTRATION

1-DAY CLASSES:

AUTO GOLD LEAFING
Gary Jenson reveals all the tips, tricks & techniques for mastering this highly profitable art.

INTRO TO PINSTRIPING
Here's the perfect initiation & prerequisite to the 4-day Pinstriping Mastery class. You'll learn drills, techniques, materials & supplies, & much more!

INTRO TO AUTOMOTIVE GRAPHICS
Recommended for beginning airbrush users as a prerequisite to the 4-day Automotive Graphics class.

INTRO TO MURALS ON STEEL
A must for beginning or "rusted" airbrush users to register in the 4-day Murals on Steel class.

OTHER 1-DAY COURSES:
INTRO TO AIRBRUSHING
PHOTOSHOP TECHNIQUES
ILLUSTRATION CHEAP TRICKS & SPECIAL F/X

Advance Your Technical Expertise:
- Experience invaluable one-on-one instruction.
- Learn the tips, tricks and techniques from general to specialized, introductory to advanced.
- View live demonstrations and presentations from top airbrush veterans.
- Test new supplies, and sample the latest products and equipment, for free!

Indulge in Extracurricular Activities:
- Use your free time to explore local attractions.
- Non-participating guests can shop and sightsee.

Build Your Business:
- Learn how to operate a successful business.
- Fine-tune your business acumen.
- Add finished pieces to your portfolio.
- Use new knowledge to earn back your Getaway investment almost immediately.

Networking Opportunities:
- Develop associations with leaders in your field.
- Expand and enhance your contact base.
- Establish friendships with colleagues.
- Gain important new insights from the unique talents of your industry counterparts.

Register today toll free:
1-800-232-8998
International: 732-223-7878
www.airbrushaction.com

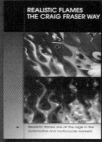

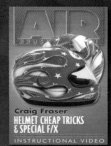
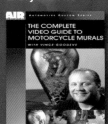

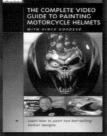

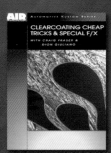
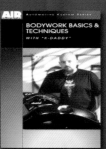